A MEMOIR

TEAM
Emily

J G WILSON

Praise for Team Emily

Life after spinal cord injury results in an unforeseen and challenging journey. My own life has been enriched by families such as the Wilsons. I see the love, courage, and perseverance that bring untold and unexpected joyful experiences and triumphs. New discoveries are happening all the time, and knowledge on how to apply them to achieve victories over paralysis is growing, so all your investing and the continued work are the path toward ongoing recovery.
—**Susan Harkema, Ph.D. Professor, Department of Neurological Surgery; Associate Scientific Director, University of Louisville**

It was a pleasure to play a part in the process of introducing Jack and Emily to my daughter Susan, and I'm happy that Emily is making significant progress.
—**Jim Harkema**

Surviving spinal cord injury is no easy task, but the support from TEAM Emily is a wonderful and realistic glimpse at how to overcome.
—**Dr. Kim Anderson**
Professor, Department of Neurological Surgery
Director of Education, The Miami Project to Cure Paralysis

The old notion that *"Life is 10 percent what happens to you and 90 percent how you react to it"* holds even more true in the circumstance of paralysis. Deep-rooted strength, faith, and courage are necessary to overcome the seemingly impossible. Emily and Jack's optimism in the face of a horrible tragedy have led to a new life of growth, prosperity, and happiness through hard work, discipline, and a never-ending desire to succeed.
—Mike Barwis, Founder & CEO of Barwis Methods companies, First Step Foundation, Athletic Angels Foundation

Team Emily provides unique insights through one family's journey of overcoming a spinal cord injury. It is informative, inspiring, genuine, and recommended for all who wish to know more about the kind of perseverance and attitude it takes to overcome disability.
—Brock Mealer

The hardest information a parent can hear is that his or her child has been catastrophically injured or worse. This is a journey of tragedy and sacrifice, giving way to triumph and love that all came together wonderfully and created an environment for Emily to recover and flourish. A beautiful story written by a father of his profound and unconditional love for his daughter.
—Tom Hoatlin

TEAM *Emily*

By Jack G. Wilson

© 2019 Jack G. Wilson

All rights reserved. No part of this book may be reproduced or transmitted in any form or by any means, electronic or mechanical, including photocopying, recording, or by any information storage and retrieval system, except in the case of brief quotations embodied in critical articles and reviews, without prior written permission of the publisher.

Although the author and publisher have made every effort to ensure the accuracy and completeness of information contained in this book, we assume no responsibility for errors, inaccuracies, omissions, or any inconsistency herein.

Printed in the United States of America.

Library of Congress Control Number: 2019933536

ISBN Hardcover: 978-1-949639-41-4

This book is dedicated to all the individuals that made "Team Emily" possible and to Emily. My awe-inspiring daughter, Emily, gave me a reason to share our journey. With abundant love for my daughter, I tell her story from the perspective of a father and a healthcare advocate.

Table of Contents

INTRODUCTION 1

CHAPTER 1 11
Preparing for the Unthinkable

CHAPTER 2 25
Insurance and Funding (Navigating Your Options)

CHAPTER 3 37
Maintaining and
Navigating Relationships after a Serious Injury

CHAPTER 4 49
Recovery Coaching

CHAPTER 5 57
Getting Up . . . Falling Down . . . and Getting Up Again

CHAPTER 6 69
Onto the Inpatient Rehab Hunt

CHAPTER 7 79
Gaining Hope from the Experts

CHAPTER 8 87
Advocating and Getting the Most from Doctors and Nurses

CHAPTER 9 95
Going Public

CHAPTER 10 105
Flying the Rehab Coop

CHAPTER 11 117
Caring for Yourself While You're Caring for Another

CHAPTER 12 129
Finding and Managing Caregivers

CHAPTER 13 137
Creating Your Care Manual

CHAPTER 14 145
Immune System and Nutrition

CHAPTER 15 153
Therapy for Life

CHAPTER 16............................ 161
Next Step to Independence

EPILOGUE............................. 171

ADDITIONAL RESOURCES 183

ACKNOWLEDGMENTS

Great appreciation and gratitude is extended to all those that impacted each and every phase of Emily's journey starting with her two siblings, Ashley and Joshua; her mother, Dana; her Uncle Steve, and his wife Susan. They kept our spirits high and optimistic when every new challenge arose. My parents, Garver and Isabelle, which Emily had such a strong connection with while living in Florida. She could always count on her grandparents as they could count on her.

My assistant, Lisa Arthur, with her kindness, compassion, and assistance making sure that I could focus on taking care of Emily without undue interruptions from my office.

My Strategic Coach instructor, Adrianne, which was the spark that influenced me to tell Emily's story. She also helped develop a strong leadership team at work and with Emily's care team.

To the healthcare teams, from nurses to doctors and everyone in-between that were so kind and compassionate during every step of the way. The therapists and trainers that took a true interest in helping her succeed, never focusing on what she could not do but what she could.

From the very beginning, her friends were with her at the most critical times when she needed them the most.

The trauma team which helped our family deal with this life changing event through empathetic and quality care. University of Michigan inpatient rehab team that gave all of us hope and comfort of what could be accomplished and how we could get there.

These relationships brought us here to the present and will be with us into the future. We are truly blessed to have been touched by these dedicated and truly caring individuals.

Our faith in God continues to be renewed every step of the way. These relationships brought us here to the present and will continue to be with us in the future.

SYNOPSIS

This is a story of great courage and drive that diminished the frustration and disappointments of a catastrophic injury. It is a story of confidence and triumph which was fueled by teamwork and relationships. Each chapter is filled with practical information that follows a chain of events with references to information and recommendations. My purpose in sharing the story of my daughter's spinal cord injury is to empower and provide you with resources so that you can support and care for your loved ones. Every step of the way, you will find a new hope that dispels the negativity surrounding catastrophic injuries. Read on to learn what to expect after a traumatic injury. Not knowing the realities of the journey you are about to travel can be a frightening and lonely experience. Become your own advocate or your loved one's advocate. Don't succumb to failures, regroup each time you are presented with a setback. Always think positively and move forward to reach your goals. You will learn what to expect—even if your motivation is to simply appreciate the lives of others such as my daughter, Emily, and her amazing team!

The Day of the Accident

Introduction

The Phone Call

It all began with a phone call.

It was the Fourth of July weekend, filled with fireworks, barbecues, and red-white-and-blue. I had just come home from a street festival in downtown Ann Arbor and was settling into my condo for a relaxing evening. My kids were all grown and off on their own. I too was on my own, and happy to enjoy the quiet of my home. If I thought of anything at all as my mind drifted toward sleep, it was that life was good.

And then came the call.

The shrill ring jolted me from my slumber. It took me a few moments before I slowly arose and picked up the receiver.

"Hello?" I said.

"Is this Jack, Emily's father?"

"Yes," I answered. I normally didn't give out my information so willingly, but there was something in the tone of the voice, which sounded familiar, but not enough to place, that made me take it seriously.

"Jack, this is your daughter's roommate Heather." She paused, searching for the words. "Emily has been in an accident. The nurse here at the hospital would like to talk to you about her condition."

Chills came over me. Any remnant of my previous daydreaming had dissolved, and now I was left stunned. I had no idea what had happened to my daughter, but I knew one thing: from the moment that phone rang, *our lives would never be the same.*

* * *

Emily had been living in West Palm Beach for close to four years. She was born a snow baby, but never quite fit the role. While she was growing up in Michigan, her dreams were always of some warmer climate with sunshine and beach, and she had finally found it.

The West Palm Beach lifestyle suited her perfectly. She was active in exercise and had fine-tuned her appearance and style. Friends and family complimented her on how great she looked, and how happy and free-spirited she seemed with life. She had just left a difficult relationship and was studying nutrition, with her eye on transferring to a four-year university. I couldn't have been more proud and happy for Emily.

Emily and I were extremely close. Emily and her mother had endured a tumultuous relationship while she was a teenager, and so she came to live with me for a few years after her mother and I divorced. When she was that age, I would have described Emily as a wild child, always testing the system for weaknesses. Once she found one, she took advantage of it.

Even as a young girl, she was both stubborn and difficult; her spirit name would be "Will of Elephant Herd." Of our three children, she tried the limits of our parenting skills, but looking back, I see that it was simply more difficult for her to discover her path.

After she moved in with me, I learned that, for the most part, she wanted someone she could talk to, someone who would listen and not judge. Once I discovered this, our relationship greatly improved. We grew close, and over the course of eight years, I felt that I was not just her confidant, but that she accepted me and understood me for who I was, too.

At twenty-six, Emily was one of those late bloomers you hear about. She was always one to learn by experience, a tendency that had given way to its own set of problems over the years. It had cost us both heartache and money, but that did not change how much I loved her and wanted her to succeed in life. After her move to West Palm Beach, she seemed to have found her path. We both thought that the difficult times were behind us, but as we would soon discover, life was about to throw us a huge curveball.

* * *

All I know of that day is what her friends were able to recall.

Emily had only been living with Heather and Lindsey for a few months, but they were fast friends. She finally seemed happy with her schedule, working part-time at a restaurant while going to school for nutrition. Those three were always planning fun activities, and the Fourth of July weekend was no exception.

The plan for the holiday was a last minute barbecue on the third before a huge Independence Day bash on a boat, along with five hundred other young patriots who loved celebrations and boating. Emily was so excited for the weekend: she had had a bathing suit made for the fourth so she could show up in style.

The day of the barbecue, Emily and her friends gathered at the apartment and rounded up the ingredients for a cookout at the pool.

Just before heading down, Heather wanted a picture of the three roommates taken. Emily , stood next to her roommates with an incredibly confident smile, ready to enjoy time with her new best friends.

They all went down to the cookout and decided to get in the pool. Her friends got in the water, sitting on the ledge in the deep end.

"Someone hold my bracelet?" Emily asked before walking to the other side of the pool. "I'm jumping in!"

She jumped in, and after a few minutes, one of the guys at the party looked down and saw something odd. It looked like Emily was goofing around, floating face down in the shallow end. But he realized something was wrong, and he called for the others to help.

At that point, Ryan, Heather's boyfriend, dove into the water and swam feverishly over to Emily. He grabbed her leg with no response and immediately carried her out of the pool and flipped her over onto her back so she could breathe. It wasn't yet clear why she was unconscious, but when he pulled her out of the water, there seemed to be something wrong with her neck.

Two other friends came over and started CPR. They weren't sure how much water Emily had aspirated, so they started compressions and mouth-to-mouth resuscitation. Heather ran over to see her. At the same time, her other roommate, one of friends started panicking and screaming uncontrollably. Other friends tried to calm her, but they were making it worse. Finally, someone grabbed her and calmed her down.

The two helping with CPR noticed that Emily still had a pulse, but she did not seem conscious. Heather noticed Emily's eyes flutter but couldn't see her breathing. It all seemed like a blur at the time.

They continued CPR for a few minutes until the EMT came rushing onto the scene.

The EMTs immediately put her neck in a brace, strapped her onto a board, and continued working on her breathing, diligently checking her pulse. Minutes later, Emily was in an ambulance speeding off to St. Mary's Trauma Center with lights and siren blaring.

Her friends followed the ambulance to St. Mary's. Once they arrived, it all seemed surreal. Emily had been taken directly to the ER, so her friends remained in the waiting room. As the hospital staff asked for information, Lindsey was able to compose herself and helped the group answer questions about what had happened.

The medical team began to stabilize Emily's vitals. The head orthopedic spine surgeon came in to assess Emily's condition. No one knew how long Emily had been in the water, and brain damage could not be ruled out. It was clear this was a life-threatening situation, but all of her friends believed that Emily, with all her stubbornness and strong will, would pull herself away from the face of death. If anyone could, it was Emily. And with the medical team at work, it was time to make the call to notify her parents.

* * *

After those first words, "Emily has been in an accident," I felt like I was in a fishbowl. My surroundings blurred into shapes and colors. Sound grew dim. After what seemed like an eternity, I snapped back to life. I had to pull it together to determine what was happening with my daughter.

Heather had seemed so calm and collected on the other end, so how bad could it be? Finally, the ER nurse picked up the phone.

"Mr. Wilson, this is Judy from the ER department of St. Mary's in West Palm Beach. I am sorry to inform you that your daughter has been in an accident that has caused paralysis. She has a compressed fracture of the C6 vertebra and has suffered a spinal cord injury. She has aspirated a significant amount of water from the accident."

What happened?

What did it mean?

"It appears to be a pool accident," she said, and began to go over the details of Emily's condition. "She has sustained a spinal cord injury and is currently in traction to take pressure off her spinal cord. She is presently experiencing quadriplegia. Her vitals are stable, but she is on a ventilator."

"What?" I cried out. "Oh God, is she going to be okay?"

There was silence for many seconds, and then the nurse continued, "She is doing well, considering all that she has been through. Will you be coming down here?"

"Absolutely," I said. "I will catch the next available flight."

I hung up the phone and began to pace, my brain scrambled with all the information I had just received. I'd scribbled down notes of what the nurse had told me, but now it all seemed garbled, as if it were part of some terrible dream.

Quadriplegia. Compressed fracture C6. Traction. Ventilator.

I had no idea what it all meant, but my mind kept leaping to all sorts of scenarios, including possible death.

I began to weep, overwhelmed with the gravity of my daughter's situation, but then I realized I had to be strong, strong for my daughter, and strong for her brother and sister, Joshua and Ashley, not to mention their mother. I collected myself, even if it seemed to last for only a few seconds before the panic returned. Ultimately, I resolved to push forward and be optimistic.

With all the strength I could muster, I began making the hardest calls of my life. I told each of my family members to be strong and that Emily would be okay. My most trusted work colleague and close friend, Lisa, found a direct flight that left at 7:30 the next morning. I continued pacing my condo for the rest of the night, attempting to pack and calm my mind from the frantic thoughts.

This is where my story begins, the story of a father's fight to care for his daughter after a catastrophic spinal cord injury resulting from a tragic accident. Within a blink of an eye, everything had turned upside down.

But this is not a story of tragedy and sorrow.

This is a story of courage, drive, along with the frustration and disappointment that comes with a catastrophic injury. This is a story of triumph and teamwork.

From the time I first got that phone call, my life was filled with questions, questions that seemed impossible to answer. When you have a loved one in a life-threatening situation, all you want is for a true understanding of the situation and for someone to step in with experience and knowledge to guide and tell you all the right decisions to make.

This is a story of courage, drive, along with the frustration and disappointment that comes with a catastrophic injury. This is a story of triumph and teamwork.

Unfortunately, it's not so simple.

The injury is only the beginning of uncertainty. Then there's the uncertainty of what your loved one's life, as well as your own, will look like. And then there's the uncertainty of medical terms and procedures, infections, health-insurance policies, legal rights, financial implications, equipment, therapy, and so much more.

When a loved one sustains a serious injury, he or she will require help and attention that you, most likely, will know nothing about. I know *I* didn't at the time. Your loved one will need a strong advocate who can speak out on his or her behalf and ask those difficult questions. Having fought through it all with my daughter, I have come out much wiser, and I'm here to share that wisdom with you.

After reading this book, you will understand more about what to expect when someone experiences a spinal cord injury or a life changing injury. You will gain insight into how to navigate it with your loved one. You will learn how to juggle your own life with this new role of care manager and caregiver that you may adopt. You will also learn how important you are in the process of recovery and how you can be an advocate and coach for your newly discovered team that will be critical in the recovery process.

Once out of the hospital, my daughter achieved milestones, from conquering different levels of therapy to achieving new abilities and everything in between. She went from the ICU to eventually learning to be more independent and live on her own, with some assistance. But it was a long journey to get there.

If you or a family member has recently experienced such a catastrophic injury, then I am here to help answer some of your questions. I am here to help guide you so that you, too, can persevere and discover that, in the face of adversity, even when the world makes no sense at all, you and your loved one can find the strength and hope to heal and discover a new life.

Hiking at Zion for LLS

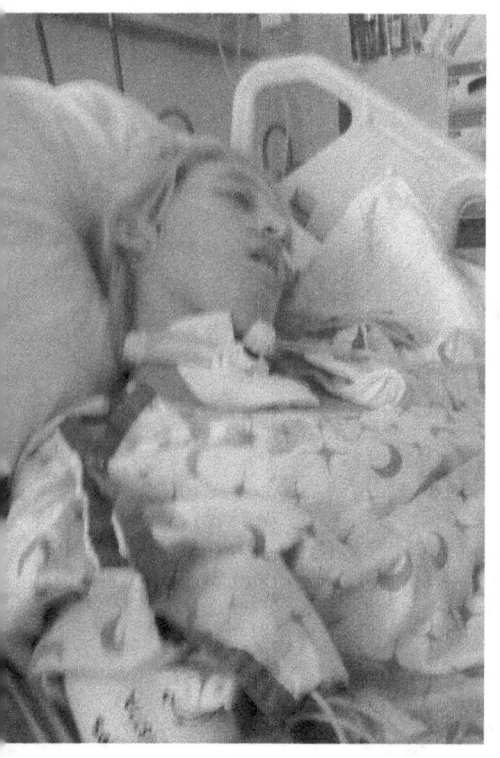

At St. Mary Hospital

CHAPTER 1

PREPARING FOR THE UNTHINKABLE

The greatest challenge after receiving news of an accident is making it to the hospital as fast as possible. I had to fly halfway across the country, but the car ride from the airport to see Emily at the hospital seemed like an eternity.

Despite my sleepless night before, my head was buzzing with questions and "what-ifs." Emily's mother flew out with me and kept circling back to the idea that it was somehow her fault, if only she had called to interrupt that moment, if only she had said something about being more careful. This is a very human reaction, especially as a parent. You want to protect your child from all harm, but the truth is, you can't.

Sometimes accidents happen, and when they do, it's hard not to rethink every moment and action leading up to the event, but what good is that? It won't change your present situation, and it certainly won't help anyone.

Instead, think of the present. You can't change the past, but you *can* influence what happens in those crucial moments after an accident when every moment counts. And in this chapter, I'll cover the most important things one can do after you get "the call".

Ask for Help

At some point, everyone experiences hardship; everyone faces a challenge that is emotionally, physically, and financially taxing. During those most difficult times in life, it's easy to forget that there are people out there who will help, who want to help.

Sometimes, just letting your situation be known allows you to move quickly and efficiently solve a problem. Your situation is not an excuse; it's a matter of fact.

When I first arrived at the airport, my flight was delayed, and then delayed again. We waited on the tarmac for an hour. I was in no mood to "stand by," so I went up to the nearest flight attendant and explained our situation. No more than five minutes later, another person from the flight crew walked up to me and informed me that the flight would likely be canceled in the next fifteen minutes, and then instructed us to deplane.

When I deplaned, the gate attendant confirmed Emily's mother and myself on the next flight out and put us in first class. Of course, first class had no meaning that day, but that act of kindness meant so much in those terrifying moments of waiting to be at Emily's side.

Not everyone was so supportive though; when we sat down, a disgruntled man came up to us and said, "You must be some high-level traveler to be upgraded in front of me."

I could only say "Sure" and look away in disbelief.

As I sat down in my seat, I made a call to the office. Lisa had already made all the necessary arrangements to get us to Emily as quickly as possible. Lisa proved to be a tremendous help which was needed to make these detailed arrangements efficiently. I suddenly realized that people sincerely want to help others in times of tragedy. Once I'd accepted this, I felt as though a huge load had been lifted off my shoulders. Do yourself a favor and allow others to be helpful to you, for you are not in a place to do it all alone.

Stay Positive

When we first arrived at the hospital, the receptionist scanned our IDs to create hospital badges for Emily's mother and myself so we could easily gain access to Emily's room. We were then taken back to the ICU and were met by a young nurse. I was in a rush just to get to Emily's room, but before we could proceed, the woman interjected.

"Just a moment," she said. "Before you go in to see her, I want you to know that she is hooked up to a lot of equipment that may shock you. She is in traction presently to keep her neck stabilized, and she is breathing on a ventilator. She is connected to many IVs and tubes, but she is not in any pain, so I need you both to stay positive in there."

Her mother started crying, and it was difficult to hold back my own tears at the thought of my daughter's life-changing situation.

"Let's see our daughter," I said.

Once we walked into the room, we saw her friends, who had been there the whole night waiting for us. Emily was awake. Her eyes caught ours, and she began to cry. The ventilator started making strange noises as she tried to catch her breath. She was fighting the machine's rhythm.

My heart was beating a mile a minute as I noticed all of the tubes running out in every direction, connected to keep her alive. I had to look away to catch myself from crying, but then I realized that she needed me to be strong.

"We love you so much," I said. "We will see that you get through this."

I wanted to know more about the accident, but in due time. At the moment, it was important just to comfort her. I learned later just how big a difference your attitude makes to a person who has experienced extreme trauma. It may sound like the most difficult thing at the time, but stay positive, especially around the *loved one*. This gives your *both of you* hope and fortitude to push through the challenges that lie ahead.

Listen and Ask Questions

After spending an hour or so with Emily, we were ushered into a very small room in the ICU to go over the status of her condition. The orthopedic doctor on the case had a strong presence and the build of an NFL football player.

To add some levity to the situation, he introduced himself and told us that our daughter was staying in a special room, the same room that former President Bill Clinton had stayed in during his knee surgery, a bit of trivia to remove our focus from the initial shock.

Although I was relieved to get some more information, my heart sank as I comprehended that this meeting would solidify the fact that my daughter had suffered a catastrophic injury and was now a quadriplegic.

He explained that it was a very significant fracture in her C5 vertebra and a compression fracture of the C6 vertebra that had caused damage to the spinal cord. The injury had left Emily paralyzed from the chest down with some bicep and wrist movement but none in her fingers or legs and feet. He said it was a "complete" injury, meaning there was very low probability that the injury to the spinal cord could be reversed and recover function; however, there was hope in that many individuals who've sustained a similar injury have been able to regain movement months after the accident. Her injury was diagnosed at the C5 level, but the doctor was hopeful that, over time, Emily could regain function to the spinal cord around C6, or even C7, which would mean that she could use her triceps and possibly her hands, allowing more independence down the line.

I asked to see the X-rays so I could know what he was talking about.

He responded reluctantly, "This will be extremely difficult for a father to see; however, it will help you understand more." He proceeded to take us into another room and, within a minute, we were looking at dozens of X-rays from every angle. It was gut-wrenching to see her vertebrae so crushed. The neck was angled back almost thirty degrees, and after I saw that, I was ready to move on. It was absolutely horrific.

There was so much information coming at me that it was impossible to keep track of it all. The doctor talked about surgery to reconstruct her vertebrae along with a special procedure to her neck so that she wouldn't have to wear a halo for an extended time around her head and neck. The two procedures he mentioned were to reconstruct the vertebrae and remove pressure from the spinal cord. The first procedure would place two rods alongside the spine that would stabilize the vertebrae around the area that had been damaged. The second was to build a cage around the front of the spine to support her neck in lieu of the halo.

The doctor went into detail about how important it was to stabilize the neck to reduce any other damage to the spinal cord. He then explained that she would need a ventilator for some time to help with breathing. He was fairly confident that with surgery and time, she would be able to wean off the ventilator. To most people, breathing seems like the easiest thing in the world, but to Emily, it would require her diaphragm to do all the work because her intercostal and abdominal muscles were no longer functional, and their recovery would take time. This scared me the most, the idea that Emily might have to be on life support for the rest of her life. I just didn't know what we were facing.

The nurse, a middle-aged woman with short blond hair and an unsympathetic voice told us that our daughter would never walk again and that for the rest of her life she'd need significant help. While this was within the realm of possibility, it was a very poor choice of words for the nurse to greet us with. First of all, I had done some research and knew that there were many different methods for regaining function. The nurse was in no position to make such a prognosis.

Second, it had been less than twenty-four hours since the accident, and this was something I was not ready to hear. To say I was unprepared to absorb this information would be an understatement. But there's no time to pause when every minute you are just worried about your loved one's survival.

It was at this time that I made the difficult decision to be privy to everything. If it had to do with Emily's medical condition, I wanted to know about it, even if it meant viewing the horrific X-rays of the damage done to my daughter's spine, which showed me that Emily was lucky even to be alive. I wanted to see and comprehend anything and everything that had to do with my daughter's injury.

Knowledge is power, and the more you know about the injury, the less mystery there is around it and the better opportunity you have to make good, informed decisions on your loved one's behalf.

Seek Information about the Injury

It took me some time to learn how to speak with doctors to get all the information I needed. For the most part, doctors will give you a general idea of what's going on, but they won't go into specific details. A lot of that work is left to you. Write down any terms that you're not familiar with and look them up later. Research the suggested procedures and make sure you're okay with that course of action ahead of time.

Regarding any device that is to be placed in the body, you should learn about the product and manufacturer before it is installed so you can see whether there are any class action lawsuits pending or potential negative outcomes. Understand what the risks and benefits are and ask questions about other procedures known to have better outcomes. Get a second opinion if you have any reservations.

In fact, as a general rule, always get a second opinion. Seek out recognized medical experts, not just the ones in front of you, if at all possible.

One of the surgeons compelled us to have an IVC (short for inferior vena cava) filter installed to prevent blood clots that could lead to life-threatening pulmonary embolisms. What I didn't know at the time was that this particular filter is irreversible. Had I known, I would have done more research and requested another option. It was a hard lesson learned, as it caused complications later on that could have been avoided.

Research will dispel many of the myths and rumors you might hear in, or outside of, the hospital. Always look for credible resources and talk to other experts locally and in other parts of the country or world for different opinions.

Search for positive prognoses related to similar injuries so you can keep your team informed and be optimistic that, with time, there are always opportunities to gain back what was lost.

Accept the Unexpected

With my work, I was used to approaching problems directly with solutions and executing decisions in a timely manner. With my daughter, there was so much to learn and absorb that I could barely keep up. I wanted to give her every chance of survival and recovery. The task was daunting.

This was nothing like work. I so wanted to immediately address the problem, but it was not up to me; it was up to a team of professionals. The first few days were touch-and-go with infections and just trying to stabilize her. It was agonizing to wait and not know what would happen during her reconstructive surgery.

Once the infections were under control, surgery was on the schedule. With less than twenty-four hours to understand the procedures and outcomes, there was only time for prayer.

I remember like it was just yesterday, talking to my daughter as they were getting her prepared in pre-op. Once the three nurses completed their preparation work, it was time to wheel her down to the operating room. Her mother and I walked next to her as they navigated the self-propelled, advanced traction bed toward the OR.

A few doors before we arrived, the surgeon showed up to talk to all of us. In a very calming voice, he told us that this was not a complicated procedure and that he had performed it many times before. He mentioned that the surgery would take around two hours for the first procedure and one-and-a-half hours for the second procedure.

The first procedure was to stabilize the back of her vertebrae. After he'd finished with that, he would come out and talk to us to let us know how she is doing.

His last words before walking off into the operating room were, "She is in the best of hands, and we will take special care of her."

Emily's mother started tearing up and went to squeeze her hand and tell her that everything would be okay; the doctor would take good care of her.

I kissed my daughter's forehead and looked her straight in the eye and said, "We love you, and the doctor will take special care of you. We will see you before you even miss us."

The OR doors swung open, and the staff wheeled her into the room. My heart seemed to calm for the moment.

Two hours passed, however, and I started becoming concerned. Before I could start thinking about what could be going wrong, the doctor came to the surgical waiting room with a smile to let us know that Emily was doing great and the procedure had gone well. They were preparing her for the second procedure, and he would be back with her in just a few minutes, once they'd finished preparing her. Her mother and I looked at each other and took a deep breath of relief.

After another two hours of waiting, the doctor came through the door again, but this time it seemed as if something was troubling him. He told us that the second procedure had gone well and that she was doing great; however, he suspected there could be a problem with the dura, which protects the spinal cord. She needed to go into another procedure room and test for any spinal fluid leakage.

We waited another couple of hours for Emily's progress with this new challenge that faced her. Once the procedure and results were in, it appeared there was nothing for us to be concerned about regarding this last procedural outcome.

It seemed like much of what we did in those days after the accident was just waiting around for the next ups and downs. It was like we were on a perpetual roller-coaster.

There were so many times when we were told how something could go, and then we found ourselves on the brink of panic when something new came up for which we were not prepared.

You can't help but imagine all of the things that could be going wrong. All you can do is remain strong, have faith and focus on what you do know. As scientific as medicine can be, it is still an art in many ways, and every individual is unique. Be prepared to be flexible and accept the unexpected. You need to realize that you have absolutely no control over the situation, so you must remain open to and optimistic about what lies ahead. Hitting those lows was extremely tough at the time, but it did give us more appreciation for those small gains in improvement with her recovery.

Keep the Circle Informed

Friends and family will want to know everything that's going on. To avoid being bombarded with phone calls and texts, make use of resources such as blogs, which can create a central repository for what's happening. I found this extremely beneficial, not only to keep everyone informed but also as therapy for myself. Each night, I would write something positive about her recovery and some of the milestones that she had made.

In addition, many of your readers will comment on your posts, giving you strength and fortitude during such a difficult time. It's nice to know that you are not alone. Once you've had a moment to reflect on the comments posted, you will be reminded of the love and care many people have for you and your loved one. Those comments helped me view our situation from another perspective, and at the same time, they strengthened my faith.

There are some blog sites that will allow you to post videos and pictures and also allow others to donate to your loved one. A word of caution: many of the free sites do not clearly state where the money goes when one donates, so if this is something in which you're interested, make sure you know all the details ahead of time.

I started using a free blog site called caringbridge.org, but soon afterward, I moved to WordPress given that it allows users to post pictures and videos and offers a dedicated place in which to donate directly to Emily. I called the site "Getwellemily," and at one point, I had more than six hundred followers reading my posts daily, with many commenting and posting prayers. I was so amazed and touched that I felt I needed to continue posting, even though I was exhausted from everything that was happening.

Use the Resources Available to You

In addition to blog sites, there are some excellent websites that provide resources to patients and their families after a catastrophic accident has occurred. The Christopher & Dana Reeve Foundation and Paralyzed Veterans of America offer free information that can help you and your family understand more about spinal cord injury and how to care for individuals who have been diagnosed. These organizations aim to reduce the uncertainty and sense of hopelessness that come with a catastrophic injury and can help connect you to a network of others who can answer questions you might have.

The world may seem like an unfamiliar place right now, but know that you are not alone. There are many people, like myself, who have been through what you're experiencing.

You have this guidebook to help you through the stages of recovery, but you also have a huge network of trained professionals and organizations that exist specifically to help people in your situation. In the next chapter, you'll learn more about how to decide which of these resources will help you during the most important step: the beginning of recovery.

Recovery Recap:

—Ask for help

—Stay positive

—Listen and ask questions

—Seek information about the injury

—Accept the unexpected

—Keep the circle informed

—Use available online resources

Heather and Emily

Poker Run Benefit

Sip and Paint Benefit

CHAPTER 2

INSURANCE AND FUNDING (NAVIGATING YOUR OPTIONS)

After Emily had her surgery, things seemed to get back on track with her recovery.

It seemed that we were in a good place until we had a visit from one of the hospital administrators asking about insurance. They knew that Emily had no medical insurance, so they were there to help guide us through the process of applying for Medicaid. It seemed to be our only option at the time, so we moved forward with the application. The only snafu was that Emily was unable to physically sign, and I did not have the legal authority to sign the documents for her. In addition, I was technically not allowed to receive any medical information about my daughter if I did not have a medical authorization document.

My only option was to create and execute both a medical power of attorney and medical authorization document so that I could sign and receive information regarding her medical affairs. This would help us make medical decisions regarding her health; it would also enable us to receive her medical records, allowing us to assist with the decision-making process. I had the talk with Emily about what this medical power of attorney meant so that she knew that I would never be able to trump any of her medical decisions, nor take any power away from her.

I reached out to my attorney in Michigan and had Lisa research Florida state law regarding how the document should be drafted. Within a few days, I had the document created and executed.

Hospitals offer wonderful lifesaving medicine and services. When a medical emergency occurs, you are simply thankful that they exist. Only after you're on the mend, and once the bills start to roll in, does it become a different story. These services may seem more like a curse as the zeros grow and you wonder, *How am I going to pay for this?*

During this time, you absolutely need to maintain your job (in fact, you may feel like you need to take on another job), and yet your time has never been stretched so thin.

I know I felt that way. The doctor's bill alone was well over six figures. Then there would be direct-care costs after she had left rehab. There were many medical costs for services that I had to find, including caregivers, equipment, and additional therapy, which were not covered by Medicaid.

As hopeless as these figures looked on paper, I was able to manage the expenses, but not entirely on my own. Medical bills can be overwhelming, but the resources you will find during this trying time are more than wonderful; they are lifesaving.

Despite the exorbitant medical fees, you can find the support you need to assist your loved one in the recovery process. This chapter will guide you through different channels you can pursue to secure that much-needed funding.

But I'm Insured . . .

Insurance is square one for juggling hospital bills, but it is not the ultimate solution.

The reality is that any spinal injury is going to require ongoing assistance in terms of therapy and equipment, and insurance will only stretch so far. Insurance was a huge part of Emily's hospital and initial recovery experience, but it certainly did not solve the problem of funding.

The best time to start exploring funding options is at the beginning of the injury. If you have coverage, now is the time to start asking questions about what you can expect from the policy. Many insurance companies do not pay for long-term therapy, so it is essential to talk to your provider to determine what insurance you might have or need to handle those needs down the road.

One of the most important pieces of information I learned was that the diagnoses can be a stopping point for additional therapy. Emily was diagnosed as a C5 Complete. The "Complete" diagnosis limited her to ongoing therapy for increased functionality.

I was deeply disappointed when I heard that my daughter was not eligible for so many other types of therapy and research, all because her probability of functional gain had been deemed "minimal." I am of the attitude that one should always focus on the possibilities, even if they seem small. By totally cutting off the opportunity to improve, these insurance companies are severely limiting the amount of recovery a patient could experience. I feel it is unjust and foolish to limit anyone by a diagnosis category. You can expect certain outcomes with a spinal injury at a certain level; however, no spinal injury is the same, and each patient's possible outcome should not be treated as equal. I think everyone should have a chance to try all forms of therapy and research if he or she so desires.

What If I'm Uninsured?

Even if your loved one does not have health insurance (Emily did not), there are channels available to help him or her afford health care. Starting with the hospital, there are social workers who understand and may be able to offer suggestions. In addition, Medicaid, will cover a patient, but it is "needs based." This means that it is based on the assets and income of the patient at the point of applying and does varies from state to state.

If permanently disabled, you may be able to apply for Medicare even if you are under sixty-five years of age. However, this process may require a two-year waiting period. It might be well worth your while in the long term, but you may have to look into other options to help make ends meet now.

Emily had no insurance, so I had to secure Medicaid for her. I utilized the hospital case manager during the hospital stay to assist with paperwork. This also influenced Emily's options in terms of where she could go for rehab. Once someone is on Medicaid, it can be difficult for him or her to find a facility for rehab out of state because Medicaid will only pay for medical assistance within the state of residence.

Another downside of Medicaid is that many providers, such as specialists, will not accept Medicaid. For example, Emily's orthopedic surgeon did not take her Medicaid, so we were left with a giant bill for both of her procedures, including everything that was associated, from the OR to the nurses and the medical devices they needed.

So what do you do when insurance just doesn't cut it and you have to pay for those exorbitant bills with your loved one's name on them?

Fear not: there are options to help pay for care, including part of those hospital and doctor bills.

State and Local Agencies

Vocational rehab agencies are one of the first places to look for in your state. These organizations often pay for assisted technology, books, tuition, and transportation expenses related to finishing education and securing employment. Some state agencies fund modifications to vehicles or homes to make them more accessible. In addition, reduced-rate transportation, supported attendant care, and discounts to some businesses can help take the pressure off the needed medical-related services. I was able to secure a reduced rate for transportation and paid attendant care from the Department of Health Services that served the county we lived in. It may not seem like much, but every little bit helps.

Negotiate

Sometimes the solution isn't more money but more compromise. Not all fees are set in stone; in fact, you may be able to negotiate medical bills and rates with hospitals, clinics, or therapists. If the hospital can't or won't negotiate, request that the staff point you in the direction of financial resources. If all goes south in the negotiations, there are other options, including community programs, private grants, and nonprofits that can assist you.

Set Up a Nonprofit

Establishing a nonprofit organization can offer a vehicle for raising funds for your loved one. One of the most common types of tax-exempt nonprofit is the 501(c)(3). The process is relatively simple, mostly filling out appropriate paperwork for the state you live in, but if possible, I recommend that you hire a knowledgeable and experienced attorney to assist you in the process.

Once the nonprofit is set up, there are many ways to host benefit drives for it. It will not just help with present costs but also will help you, and others, afford long-term care. Plus, these donations are tax-deductible. A nonprofit can also become a lasting legacy for future patients in need.

Utilize Social Media and the Community

Social media practically runs the world and can be the backbone of funding for your cause. Facebook and Twitter will allow you to get the message out regarding important events and updates. Blog sites are also great places to spread the word, including WordPress, which, as I mentioned, I used. There is also a relatively new phenomenon called "crowdfunding," offered through sites such as GoFundMe and The Funding Source, which will allow you to set up an account wherein to accept donations. These websites have been the gateway for growing charities that support wonderful causes such as stem cell research, therapy, and equipment needs, and they can help you out in a huge way too.

There are some sites that specialize in developing community-based fundraising campaigns for people with unmet medical-related expenses due to catastrophic injuries and illnesses. There may even be local agencies in your area. Ask around or contact community organizations in your area to see whether there are grants available or options that can assist in paying bills.

Plan a Benefit

Most everyone likes to attend a benefit to help others; use this to your advantage. Shortly after Emily had had her accident, her friends planned a boating poker-run benefit and a beer pong tournament. Both were a hit, and they really helped support Emily emotionally during those early days. I owe it all to Emily's friends who did all the planning and even set up the event! We ended up using the funds to purchase a new wheelchair with power wheels (which was not covered by insurance).

Research available resources that can help you set up the event. Know a lot of people who like to play golf? Organize a tournament! Have a favorite local band? Throw a concert benefit!

Contact local businesses to see whether they might allow you to use their facilities for the benefit. You can even sell wristbands or T-shirts to promote the event. I ended up promoting both of these on WordPress to help fund Emily's therapy. Big or small, on your front lawn or at a concert hall, an event will bring your community together and help out a person everyone cares so much about. You can even make this an annual event.

Research Products and Therapy Trials/Studies

Being a participant in a study can sometimes work in your favor, especially when it comes to new recovery methods. In some cases, in return for participating, you are entitled to compensation during the study.

After undertaking extensive research and testing, labs turn to human subjects to undergo final trials for their cutting-edge products. Compensation varies, but depending on the study, you could even be approved to receive income from the process, along with a possible benefit related to recovery of function.

Your participation all comes down to what you feel comfortable with. As with anything, research will guide you in determining whether a study will benefit your patient in the long run or pose too great a risk. Perform due diligence before making a decision.

Research Grants

Many grants are available for different types of assistance, including therapy and care, which can help defray the costs of some of the initial programs your loved one will go through. Resources such as the Center for Independent Living in your area can help connect you to possible grants for equipment, support groups, and other physical needs.

Emily was fortunate enough to receive a grant for therapy from the Recovery Project. This was only supposed to last three months; however, it was extended to six months. This was her first advanced therapy that increased her endurance and helped her gain significant confidence in her ability toward independence.

Don't Be Afraid to Ask

You may feel uncomfortable about the idea of asking friends, family, or new acquaintances for money or help (I know I do), but it's something you just may have to get used to. Perhaps it will make you feel better to know that, through my experience, I realized there are so many people out there who would love to help in many different ways; you simply have to be willing to ask. Because if you don't ask, how will they ever know you need help to begin with?

Ask family and ask friends. Ask companies that may have a product that would benefit your loved one. You can ask individuals to donate a couple of hours to stay with your loved one while you run errands. I sent many letters to companies asking for help, both personally and through Emily's blog site. I was very successful in securing many types of assistance, and to this day, I cannot imagine what it would have been like if I had not received that help.

Bottom line, you have to ask. Regardless of how much money and time you have, it's almost impossible to bear all of it on your own. The emotional, financial, and physical toll is real. You will get through it, and in time the gratitude you feel for all that you and your loved one have accomplished will make you feel downright triumphant, but you won't get there without a team by your side. So ask, and be prepared to put that team to work!

> *Bottom line, you have to ask. Regardless of how much money and time you have, it's almost impossible to bear all of it on your own.*

Recovery Recap:

—**Establish insurance and determine limits**

—**Research state programs and those of local agencies**

—**Negotiate fees with providers**

—**Set up a nonprofit**

—**Research community-based fundraising**

—**Utilize social media and the community**

—**Plan a benefit**

—**Research product and therapy trials/studies**

—**Research grants**

—**Don't be afraid to ask others for help**

Nephew Gives Emily a Push

Gail Makes a Visit

CHAPTER 3

MAINTAINING AND NAVIGATING RELATIONSHIPS AFTER A SERIOUS INJURY

It was miraculous to see how many friends and family members turned up in Emily's hospital room each day after the injury, sometimes more than twenty at a time. Most of these people she had only met within the few months since she had moved to Florida. Their help was nothing short of amazing.

Her friends came around the clock to be with her and offered their support in so many ways. One of her roommates brought in a portable blow-up washbasin so she could wash and style Emily's hair and do her nails. Another brought in food practically every night so we could stay at the hospital with Emily. And then came the cards, flowers, and prayers that never seemed to end, even from the family of other patients in the ICU.

Then there was Don and his dog, Pollyanna, who came multiple times a week. Don had a C6/7 level of injury and had the same orthopedic surgeon as Emily. Don, an administrator on staff, shared a wealth of information and was so helpful to all of us.

Many nights, Emily's friends brought in dinner for the family. Poor Emily couldn't sample even a morsel of food. She was on a ventilator, which meant that all food, other than the liquid nutrients the hospital gave her through her NG tube (feeding tube), was off-limits.

Her friends would try to lighten the mood by joking about the dried-out hospital chicken, but we could tell Emily missed even that. It would be weeks, or maybe months, before she could eat a regular meal, at which point, fast-food had the appeal of a 5-star restaurant. Even drinking water was totally off the menu, and Emily banned many of us from bringing in bottled water to the room, especially me.

Hospitals have firm restrictions on how many people can be in the patient's room at one time (ours was eight), but there were certain nurses who would grant us leeway when Emily's crowd gathered.

Oftentimes, though, the family would have to sit out in the waiting room in the evenings to make way for all her friends. It touched each of us to see the love they had for Emily, and by extension, our family. There was always someone offering to stay with her so we could take a break, but in those early days, it was tough to leave her alone.

If your loved one lives in or is staying in a hospital in another state, simply maintaining a living situation close by can be an issue. I really wanted a place where the family could reside, along with any other visitors who wanted to see Emily. Some trauma hospitals may have short- and long-term housing close by for people in this very situation.

I learned of such a place from our new friend Don. This residence offered low rates to families that needed to be with their children who were in the hospital. The beautiful seven-room home had a large kitchen, screened-in porch, and game rooms built to be accessible by those with limited or impaired mobility.

For the most part, these living units are offered under special conditions, but sometimes it really is the squeaky wheel that gets the grease. I persisted in requesting the residence, and thanks to the help of our new friend Don, we were finally approved. It was the best situation for all of us and allowed the family an opportunity to talk to other parents about normal things, giving us a break from the drama.

I ended up giving the room to Emily's mother so she could be more comfortable. I stayed at a local hotel. This allowed us to be in a position to take care of Emily in shifts and allowed some of her friends, who had diligently stayed by her side while we went to and from our sleeping quarters, to regenerate back at our rooms.

It always amazed me that, even when Emily didn't feel well—even on the nights she was most depressed—she would search for that inner strength to perk up for visitors. She cares so deeply for her friends and family and knew that if one person was down, then it was likely that the rest of the visitors in the room would feel the same, so she would try her hardest to keep a smile on her face and suppress those feelings of sadness that were just unavoidable. It was the one thing that truly seemed to put a sparkle back in her eye. She could be having the most challenging day ever, but if she knew someone was coming to visit, she would perk herself up and shoulder through. These visits were helpful for the family in strengthening our hope as well as dealing with the difficulties of the situation.

Friends and family mean everything in a time of crisis. It's a classic lesson learned during life's most difficult trials and travails, but what you don't realize at the onset of such challenges is just how much those relationships will change over the course of the injury, rehabilitation, and healing process.

As your loved one navigates this new phase in life, some relationships will grow stronger, some people who were close may become distant, and plenty of new friendships will form, too.

As difficult as it may be for your loved one to adapt, it's similarly difficult for those friends and family members to know how to handle these changes as well.

First, there's the issue of simply being with the person after his or her injury. How do you talk to someone who might not be able to respond?

Then there is the difficulty of knowing what to say. What do you say to someone who has been through a traumatic experience?

What's okay to talk about, and what's not okay?

And finally, once your loved one is out of the hospital, how can you prepare him or her to meet new people out in the real world?

There are so many questions, many of which can only be answered in time. Just as every injury is unique, so is every patient's healing process. But I will tell you that, regardless of the person, the people who are active in their loved one's life right now will make all the difference in the healing process.

Whom Should I Let In?

You may feel reluctant to allow certain visitors, but ultimately, you have to let your loved one decide for him or herself whom he or she wishes to see.

We all think that our kids are vulnerable, even after they've become adults. I certainly struggled with the instinctive impulse to protect my daughter. During her stay in the ICU, I noticed a new visitor start to show up, often at the end of the day, just before we left. As it turned out, it was someone she had gone out with before the injury. They hadn't spoken in a while, and suddenly he seemed to want to be back in her life.

I felt so conflicted. Emily clearly seemed to enjoy his company, but at the same time, the situation was disconcerting. It may have been harmless, returning after a life-changing event to his old friend, but how could he possibly fathom how this would affect Emily in the long run? Was he mature enough to handle all of the challenges ahead? Was he aware of how vulnerable she was presently?

As much as I wanted to tell this guy to back off, it was my daughter's choice. All I could do was talk to him. I told him about the injury and explained how much her life would change because of it. I hoped that by my being very clear about Emily's needs and state of mind, he would honor and respect the delicacy of their relationship. Unfortunately, it turned out as I had suspected: a couple of months after her hospital stay, he got a new girlfriend and disappeared.

It took some time for Emily to recover from the emotional blow, never mind the injury. As her parent, I simply wanted to make her feel better, but in retrospect, I know there is nothing more I could have done. It's a good idea to brief any visitors, and those close to the injured patient, on what the patient is going through, but in the end, you have to let your loved one set the pace.

How Should Visitors Behave?

In the beginning, it's incredibly difficult to know how to act around someone with a recent catastrophic injury. The patient might be connected to all kinds of intimidating equipment with tubes and wires, not to mention, the monitors and sounds that fill the room, and he or she may not look quite like his or her former self.

Emily was on a ventilator, so she couldn't speak. That did not seem to affect communication with her friends; however, to help us communicate better, we used a whiteboard and wrote things down that we thought she was saying. When we found out that was less than effective, her sister, Ashley, created an ingenious picture board with a few basic words, which became our method for much better communication. Her brother, Joshua, was a pillar of strength; however, some friends who visited her were clearly uncomfortable with the gravity of the situation. Some would go in and tear up just about every time. It's an understandable reaction; after all, this person you care so deeply about is in a daunting situation. I will tell you that your tears will help no one, not even yourself, and certainly not the injured person.

If you are the primary person in the hospital with him or her, it will be your responsibility to give visitors a pep talk before seeing your loved one. Their reaction will tell the patient whether he or she should feel confident that everything is going to be okay. Tell the patient positive things regarding prognosis and how there are many reasons to celebrate his or her life. In many ways, we were lucky to have Emily alive, and I was not shy about telling her that.

Have a conversation with the visitors. Tell them to remember to stay positive, to be glad to see him or her, and to talk to the patient like a regular person. Acknowledge that it's hard on the visitors, but make it clear that signs of grief make it harder for the patient, too. If someone has a difficult time controlling his or her emotions, don't hold it against that person. Don't ban him or her from coming. Just continue to coach that individual on how to turn his or her behavior around. Be optimistic and show your strength and always remember to smile.

What Should I Talk About?

This is one of the most common questions friends and family asked during Emily's recovery process, and the answer is incredibly simple: talk to them about normal stuff.

Just talk to her like she's the person you've known all along. Because she is.

At the same time, there is a certain tact required here. Obviously, you don't want to emphasize the fact that she's missing out because she is confined to her hospital room. Nor do you want to talk about activities you'll do that she may not be able to experience again. Beyond that, don't feel reluctant to just have a regular conversation.

If you still find it difficult to find a topic of conversation, you can keep it simple. You can say, "Hi." You can recognize something around her. You can recall a memory. You can even ask her (if she can answer), "What does it feel like?"

What people don't get is that, when you experience a serious injury, part of the burden is simply not being able to explain your situation. In Emily's case, she remembered nothing about the accident, so there was nothing to explain. Because she was on a ventilator in the ICU, I acted as the intermediary until her friends adapted to asking her yes-

and-no questions so she could simply nod or shake her head in response.

As soon as an injury occurs, it suddenly becomes a taboo subject. Perhaps this isn't the case with those whom you are close to, but once your loved one returns to the world outside the hospital, it will become evident that not everyone knows how to handle being around a person who has sustained a catastrophic injury.

No one wants to ask what happened or other questions pertaining to her physical health because he or she is afraid of making the patient feel upset or sorry about her situation.

You may be surprised to learn that, for the most part, those who have experienced injuries would actually prefer to be asked about what has happened to them. It's certainly better than staring. If the subject is uncomfortable, your loved one will certainly show signs that he or she would prefer to move on, and you can be sure to help with transitioning to the next subject.

When my daughter was discharged from the hospital, she had to get used to the way people now viewed her. They would stop and stare, but rarely would anyone ask about why she was in a wheelchair, presumably because everyone thought it would be discourteous. Truly, you offend the person more by not saying anything and instead, simply staring.

If you ever find yourself in this position, give that person the opportunity to talk about his or her situation. Talking about it normalizes what he or she is going through and affords him or her the chance to feel like a regular person.

What *Shouldn't* I Talk About?

Shortly after Emily entered the hospital, I started a blog to update our network on Emily's progress. It was great because, in addition to written updates, we could post pictures and receive comments from friends and family. We eventually formed an evening ritual of reading comments left by visitors to the site.

It would take a long time to get through them at first, as Emily tired quickly in the early post-injury days. Of course, she was also experiencing strong emotions from the heart and soul that would be amplified by the messages. At the same time, however, some comments would stop her in her tracks. It was then that I learned that even people who intended to be kind and share thoughtful words could ultimately be incredibly hurtful.

Any show of support is helpful. And again, most topics are not off the table when it comes to your loved one's condition. But here is the number one worst thing you can say to an injured person:

"I'm so sorry for you."

It's okay to feel sorry, but there is a fine line between pity and empathy. Humans appreciate empathy but are shamed by pity. No one wants to be pitied. Pitying a person makes that person feel "less than." While the person's life is certainly different, a person recovering from a traumatic injury is in no way "less than."

The mentality is that people feel sorry for you because you are broken. Well, your loved one is *not* broken, nor does he or she want to feel broken. In fact, they will be able to do some of the things they used to be able to do. So, when you talk to your loved one, remember the person they are, not the injury sustained. The number one rule is to be empathetic, and not show pity.

You Need a Friend, Too

You may not realize it now, but in time, you'll find that your greatest support comes from the new people you meet at the hospital, the other patients and family members who are going through a similar life-changing event. I met many families in the hospitals and rehab programs Emily went through, many of whom became good friends to both of us.

You'll notice that you see a lot of the same families again and again. Keep in mind that each injury is unique and that comparing notes can sometimes lead to frustration. At the same time, it is a huge relief to have someone to talk to who's experiencing a similar traumatic event and figuring out a way to get through it all.

By forming a network, you are setting both you and your loved one up for success. And now that you have a better understanding of what your loved one might need emotionally, you can help empower those around you to give extra strength and support along this journey.

One of the greatest networks we set up was with Don and his wife, Sally. Sally, an RN, was actively involved in Don's care, and we learned so much from both of them. When I first met her, she said one of the most profound things to me: *"You have been chosen to join a club in which you would never have wanted to be involved. Once in it, you will be glad you are part of it."*

That was so right on. Our club members are working together as a team, helping each other support the cause "to gain further independence and find solutions to make our lives easier." It seems like a momentous task, but with all of us working together, we can succeed.

Recovery Recap:

—**Don't be afraid to ask questions**

—**Show empathy and not pity**

—**Coach visitors on how to interact**

—**Expand your support team**

—**Join the club and work together**

At the Big House U of M Football Game

Navigating through U of M Crowd

CHAPTER 4

RECOVERY COACHING

Just as you feel a sense of relief once you realize your loved one will survive, unknowns and worries of what may happen next come rushing in. It will seem as if these ups and downs will never end, but push yourself forward to become more knowledgeable about the injury and focused on the recovery.

Research can teach you about those who have made great progress in their recovery while, at the same time, incite unnecessary terror about what "could be." This is when friends, family, and loved ones can support those positive prognoses and instill confidence in your recovery coaching and in your loved one.

This is the beginning of the long road to recovery coaching.

There will be times when you feel like an antagonist, like you're being too mean or too hard. The reality is that the goal of recovery is to help the patient regain independence. A lot of that recovery depends on how hard the patient pushes him or herself. When he or she feels depressed or experiences anxiety or grief about everything that's happening in a life that is out of his or her control, it can be hard for one to find the motivation to start that process. The beginning can feel like a helpless place.

The best way you can help your loved one is to remain their champion, but also to allow for them to help themselves by being their coach.

For several weeks after the injury, Emily was not allowed liquids by mouth due to her ventilator. As a result, her mouth would become extremely dry. The only way she could have water was by dipping a small sponge attached to a stick into water and placing it in her mouth. Almost hourly, Emily would request more water, and either her mother or I happily obliged, eager to do anything to make her more comfortable.

At the time, we had a wonderful nurse who was young and vibrant and had a way of speaking to Emily that put her at ease. The two of them just seemed to connect, I think because Emily recognized the nurse's confidence and strength, and that seemed to transfer over to Emily.

One day, the nurse was in the room when Emily asked for more water. The nurse picked up the sponge stick, stuck it in her hand splint, and said, "It's time you do it."

I was taken back by her boldness but curious to see what would happen next. I could see by her face that Emily may have felt the same. She struggled with the stick for a moment and then slowly brought it to her mouth. After a few tries, she made it in. The smile and awe on her face elicited the first glimmer of joy I had felt since the phone call on the third of July.

It was the mark of her first step in the long road ahead toward independence. At once, she realized that she would be able to do things on her own in the future, but it would take a lot of work to get there. *This was my first exposure to an individual who was a natural recovery coach.* This was the necessary approach for Emily to be successful in her recovery.

So, what's next? I wondered. *Where do we go from here?*

I was ready to get started on recovery, confident that my daughter's iron fortitude would see her through. But I had no idea how it all was supposed to happen.

One of the greatest difficulties for me was watching Emily struggle on the ventilator. The sound of strange beeps and alarms when the machine took over the pace of her breathing always sent chills down my spine.

A few weeks after the injury, I watched the numbers and graphs and listened to the noises that gave my daughter life support. It was unnerving. I was told that it might be hard to get her into any inpatient rehab program if she continued to be on the ventilator, but the news didn't worry me. I had faith that Emily would be able to progress and breathe on her own again.

However, the infections due to all the pool water she had aspirated were slowing down her recovery. I was told pool water is one of the worst substances you could have in your lungs. We remained optimistic that her immune system and the antibiotics would fight off the infections. It finally came to pass, and the weaning process was in effect.

I stayed optimistic and so did my daughter and in the fourth week of recovery, the respiratory therapist commenced the weaning process. Watching Emily struggle trying to breathe on her own during short intervals was very difficult, but I knew she would pull it off. The therapist was patient and extremely supportive of Emily's slow progress, knowing all along that in due time he could coach her off the ventilator. He never seemed to lose focus on this.

I began to become more knowledgeable about the ventilator and all its settings, readings, and graphs. I became less concerned once I could understand it more and had learned that it was assisting her breathing, not providing full function for her to breathe. I started to see the light at the end of the tunnel as her diaphragm was doing more and more of the work. Once I became more knowledgeable, I became confident that she would indeed breathe on her own at some point.

The medical team performed a tracheotomy to assist her to breathe with the ventilator in the early stages of her injury. At the point at which it was able to disconnect the ventilator to the tracheostomy, she spoke for the first time in many weeks. Her first words were, "What do you want me to say?" Hearing those words gave me such joy and happiness, but we were just getting started. Right after that we called her sister and Emily sang *Happy Birthday* to her. A week later, she came off the ventilator completely. I was never so happy or proud.

Food and drink were now back on the menu, and with that, her first request was a hamburger and fries. Within six weeks of entering the hospital, Emily was breathing on her own. Without the medical staff coaching her along, we never would have made it there.

I realized that it was coaching that would help her progress and fortify her to become more independent. The team continued to build, with mentors all around us. We were all seeing amazing results. Being that coach with so much positive influence, I was convinced that nothing could get in her way.

Practice Positive Influence

It's scary not knowing exactly what's ahead of your loved one on his or her road to recovery. Regardless of the circumstances, a positive attitude always wins. Try your best to focus on the positives and educate yourself when you encounter moments of fear or confusion concerning his or her medical state.

Begin to research positive outcomes of similar injuries on the internet. Fine-tune your findings and seek examples of patients with similar injuries who have significantly improved function so you can share their stories with your team. In the early days, nothing is a greater motivator than hope, and you and your team can influence that hope for everyone.

Coaching for Recovery

You could be the father, mother, sibling, friend, or spouse. Regardless of your role, someone will be at the helm of the ship for helping your loved one recover. In addition to positivity, this requires a coach-like mentality. What does a coach do? He or she helps you become your best self. Sometimes that process is difficult. Often it is exhausting and hurts, but sometimes it's exhilarating. A good coach helps push through those trying times with encouragement and dedication.

Empower Your Team

To succeed, the first step for me was to immediately empower my daughter to make the ultimate decision on what the next steps would be and at what pace she was comfortable with. As I stated in previous chapters, recovery is not linear, and it's really up to your loved one to decide how fast and far he or she can go. If you try to control the outcome, vested interest is limited with your loved one, and then disappointment can set in.

For me to succeed, I needed help from others. It was like things just fell into place for us, as everyone close to her had a role and purpose to help her get back to her life. What I had to do was continue to recruit those who could help and then empower them. Being a father and a coach is not easy, but having many caring assistant coaches positively influenced Emily's recovery and certainly made me feel great!

Recovery Recap:
—**Practice being a positive influence**

—**Coach for recovery**

—**Empower your loved one**

—**Don't try to control the outcome**

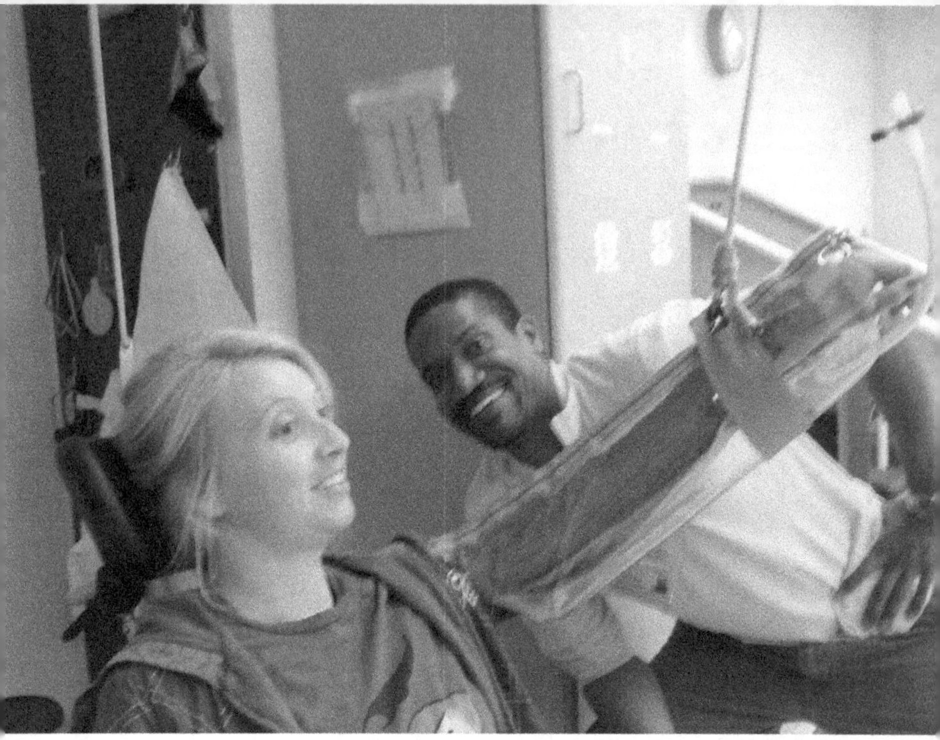

Working with PT at UMHS Rehab

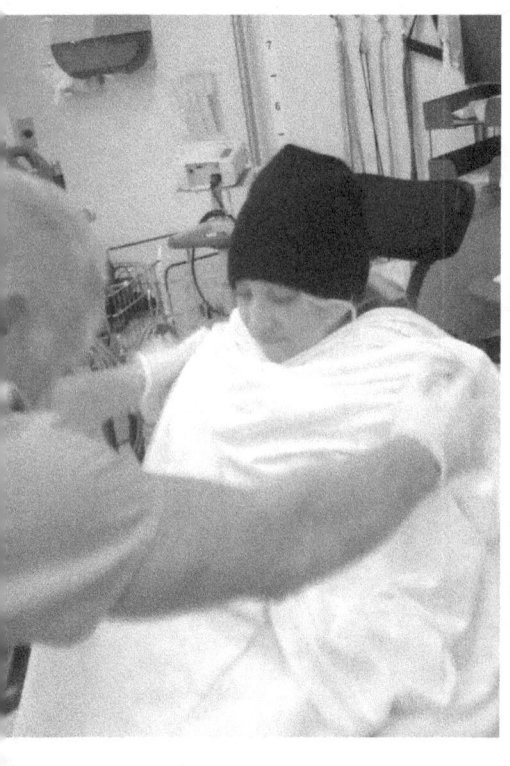

Emily at Rehab Always Cold

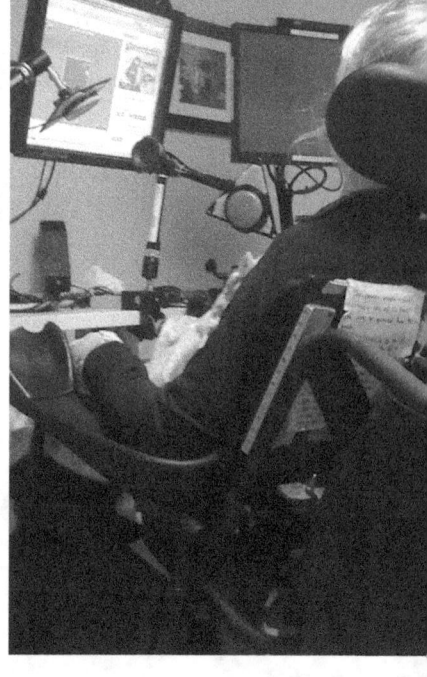

Rehab at UMHS

CHAPTER 5

GETTING UP ... FALLING DOWN ... AND GETTING UP AGAIN

From the moment I got the phone call to this very day, there have been many triumphs and challenges throughout Emily's recovery. In the world of rehabilitation, progress after a spinal cord injury is not a linear track. Some weeks, you'll chart success; in others, you will feel as if you've fallen a few steps back. Slowly, over time, you will find that the gains accumulate. Those achievements will make you and your loved one feel prouder than you've ever felt before in life. Having the stamina to make it from the peaks to the valleys and back again, that, my friend, is the real challenge.

After several long weeks in the ICU, Emily was finally moved to a step-down room. At this point, she couldn't wait to be up and about. Of course, the process wasn't quite so simple. She used a "standing frame," a bed that could be moved into multiple positions to simulate standing. The first time Emily shifted to a standing position at 75 degrees, her blood pressure dropped, and she nearly fainted. Her body struggled to regulate her blood pressure, so this became the greatest obstacle between Emily and mobility.

Every day, we worked with her by stretching her limbs and working on her range of motion. We had learned exercises while she was still at the hospital, and there were no limitations on how much she should do. I would help her with as much as she could handle, exercising both arms and legs twice a day for almost twenty minutes each, along with stretching her legs, fingers, and feet. We felt that this could also help her blood pressure gain some stability when she went back to the standing frame.

Little by little, she started to adjust to the standing frame in a semi-vertical position. The day finally came when Emily decided to take her first trip outside in the standing frame, and I was her proud escort. We found a nice spot in the sunshine, and just as I found my spot beside her, she started to feel extremely nauseated, so we quickly made it back inside.

Later that week, after continuing to practice with the standing frame, she was ready to try another trip outside her room, to venture out into the sun again. Her blood pressure was normalized, and the frame was now semi-vertical, ready to go. Our first stop was the coffee shop to show her off and then down to the ICU to say hello to some of the friends she had made during her stay there. At last, we were outside in the warm, sunny weather. She was doing great, and for the next fifteen minutes, we enjoyed the warmth of the sun and said very little. What a great day it was.

I had been out to that front entrance many times for a coffee and a breath of fresh air, but I felt like I was experiencing the outdoors for the first time through Emily's eyes. I watched as Emily sighed and closed her eyes, feeling the sun beat down on her head. It was a glorious feeling after so many days indoors, but it didn't last long. Her body struggled to maintain constant blood pressure and to control her temperature. That glorious sun was also overheating her body. I gave her some water to drink, but it didn't seem to give her any relief, so we quickly went back to the room.

Although it didn't last long, it was significant progress and showed us that with dedicated efforts came payoff. It also happened to coincide with a visit from a few of her favorite people; her grandparents from Florida, and her uncle Steve from Michigan. I went down to meet them as the nurse helped Emily with her bowel program and catheterization back in the room. I gave the family a brief tour of the facilities to kill some time, but after nearly half an hour, it seemed as if the process was taking too long. We went outside the room, and I knocked on the door.

"Just about done," the nurse called. The door opened a few moments later, and the nurse exited. I went in first to let Emily know that her family was there to see her, but then I noticed something very concerning: Emily looked as if her body was trembling. Within seconds, the tremors turned into all-out shaking and flailing as her eyes rolled back into her head. She was having a seizure.

I grabbed her arms and hands to prevent her from injuring herself and called out for the nurse while jamming the call button. The first nurse on the scene pressed the "Code Blue" button and instructed the family to leave the room. I continued to hold Emily so she wouldn't hurt herself and kept track of the time that she was in seizure.

It was a horrible thing to witness, my daughter reacting so violently to something that was out of her control, especially after such a triumphant day. I was glad I was there to protect her and keep her calm.

Once she was out of the seizure, the room was filled with nurses and doctors.

"What's going on?" I demanded. No one could tell me anything. All I could do was clear the room so they could perform tests and take vitals.

Later, in the hallway, I was told that the anxiety medication Emily was on can cause seizures as a side effect if the patient is taken off it too quickly. The doctor told me that the hospital would increase her dosage and wean her off slowly, although that didn't give me the relief I was seeking. Was it really the medication? Why, then, did it happen right after her bowel program? Or after her venture in the sun? And how could I be sure it wouldn't happen again?

I always felt these "mishaps" were protected by excuses, but what could I do? I had to accept what they told me until I could prove otherwise. There will be missteps along the way. It will be up to you to stay in step with all treatments and tasks, and say "yes" all along the way. Ask questions and keep track of all the information so you eliminate concerns and your worries.

Life went on, and we continued to work on our recently learned stretches and range-of-motion exercises until she was transferred to an inpatient rehab in Michigan.

The rehab center Emily was in had technology that taught patients how to build strength in their affected arm(s) by using a mouse on a bracket that would allow their arm to move in certain directions. Emily was actually playing a game in the process of moving her hand to utilize her arm and wrist. This was one therapy that Emily really took to. I'd sit beside her and watch her practice her skills using her arm strength. I was so proud of her progress after weeks of training that I pulled out my phone to record her work. While I had her on camera, she suddenly stopped what she was doing. I put down my phone and saw that the tremors had started back up. The shaking and rolling eyes soon followed, and I realized she was having another seizure.

Again, I did all I could to keep her calm and stable, and I called for help. One person yelled for oxygen, and a tank was rushed over, but it didn't have a mask or connections. After a few minutes passed, Emily went limp, and it seemed as if she was not breathing, which became characteristic of these episodes. The medical team stabilized her, and we ultimately received a vague diagnosis similar to the one provided us after the first seizure.

The doctors ended up putting her on an anti-seizure medication, which made her very tired and groggy. This fatigue affected her progress, so she decided to stop taking it, against the doctors' orders. That would be our Emily, for she had no problem questioning a course of action that caused an interruption to her recovery. This was a true godsend knowing that she would be questioning her course of action if she felt that it would not be beneficial for her.

Emily's body was so sensitive to medications and physical changes that we came to be prepared for these unexpected results. At some point, we had to accept that we couldn't necessarily explain or control everything, but if we were prepared and had a procedure in place for addressing the issues, then we could rest somewhat assured, knowing that in the long run, she would be okay.

Many days later, after we had left the rehab facility and were living in my condo in Michigan, another new level of awareness developed. Emily was finally taking time to understand her body and her condition, thus she was becoming more responsible and aware of her health, which made my life a little easier and less stressful.

As Emily became accustomed to the new sensations in her body, she started to notice a difference within herself, and unfortunately, it caused concern. Emily became aware that she was sweating on one side of her neck, but not the other. Soon after, she noticed her breathing had become labored. Was she experiencing autonomic dysreflexia? I checked her for any issues regarding bowels, bladder, and pressure sores as I had been taught, but couldn't find the source of the stress. At the time, it seemed likely it would go away, as there had been other times of discomfort, and because the caregiver was there, I went to work and let them know to call me if anything changed.

Soon after I had left, Emily noticed that her legs were swelling. She relayed the information to me by text. I had been through so many of these issues with Emily that this detail seemed minor to me at the time. I had the caregiver check Emily's blood pressure, and she found it was a little on the high side, but that could have been because Emily was stressed out about her symptoms. I decided that if her condition worsened, we would get her to the ER to have it diagnosed.

We soon learned that she was indeed experiencing autonomic dysreflexia, or AD, a serious condition that could lead to stroke or death if untreated. AD is a syndrome that affects individuals with a spinal cord injury above the mid-thoracic level. It's characterized by hypertension, bradycardia, and severe headaches and is the result of impaired function of the autonomic nervous system caused by simultaneous sympathetic and parasympathetic activity. It was definitely something to watch out for, but at the time, everyone was unsure what was causing her discomfort.

Around noon, I got a call from Emily, whose blood pressure was now over 160. It was time to get her to the ER. The caregiver would put her in her wheelchair and drive her to the hospital right away. I hoped we would find out the cause of her AD immediately. But I was about to learn that AD is different for everyone, and there is a signature trace of symptoms that pertained to a certain issue with my daughter.

When I arrived at the ER, I checked in and found Emily. It was a Friday afternoon, and the ER was getting busier. It took several requests before she was placed in a large procedure room and was brought some warm blankets to make her more comfortable. Still, we had no idea what was causing this.

Finally, the cardiovascular team came into the room, which was something of a comfort, but not completely. Through all that we had experienced, I learned that some symptoms cannot always be pinpointed and diagnosed—proof that art meets science, in my mind.

I found that even in the medical profession, not everyone really understands how to care for a quadriplegic. If he or she is moved or positioned in a certain way, it could cause harm or discomfort such as AD to the individual, and most of the medical staff were fearful of her condition. All the more reason to stay at her side as they scanned her legs. She became very comfortable with my understanding of how to move and position her due to my experience and understanding of her condition.

To my horror, I watched as the radiologist identified blood clots in her legs and marked each in size and position as it was recorded. She had a massive number in her right leg, which always seemed colder than the left. Before I thought it was just a blood circulation issue, but now I saw that it was serious. After the radiologist finished identifying the clots, we were back in the hallway waiting for more information.

An hour went by, and the doctor came back in with some answers. Emily had suffered significant blood clots in both legs due to the IVC filter that was close to 85 percent obstructed. (Remember the tip about researching procedures before they take place? Well, this is why.)

The IVC filter, the doctor told us, was a real setback. The nonretractable filter was originally put in place to reduce any blood clots going into the lungs that could cause pulmonary embolisms. The good news was that it had done its job; however, in the course of working, it had also become obstructed, which slowed the blood flow out of the legs and had created a significant number of blood clots.

Emily looked up at me in disbelief. I just dropped my head, scared to hear what would come next.

"What can we do now?" I asked.

The only solution available was a medication that would increase the viscosity of her blood. Some of the clots would stabilize, whereas others could dissolve. She would need shots in her abdomen for two months, followed by medication that she would take for the rest of her life.

Another two steps back, I thought, although outwardly, I had to stay strong for my daughter. As I had told my daughter from the beginning, we would get through this, and I would make sure that she would be okay, but as of this moment, it really concerned me. What would this new diagnosis mean for her health? Would I need to be concerned with her bleeding out with an injury or having a stroke? I already had multiple caregivers, along with the team of nurses, doctors, and therapists helping her. How much more could I do for my daughter? How could I help her handle more crises?

When I finally got home, it was late, but I was able to sleep through the night because my daughter was being cared for at the hospital. When I woke up, I was certain it was all a dream. I ran to my daughter's bedroom, and when I saw the empty bed, the illusion disappeared. I grabbed a coffee and went to spend another day with Emily at the hospital.

Emily remained in the hospital a few more days, enough for another couple of restful nights of sleep. As with all the other changes that happened after the accident, we learned to deal with this latest development. It's so hard to accept new medical challenges after a traumatic accident; when they arise, you may find yourself asking, *How can I possibly take on any more? How much more can I give? How much more can I help my loved one fight through this?*

The answer is that, when it comes down to it, you do what you have to do. And you adapt. Over time, as you get more practice, you, and those around you, realize just how strong you really are. I believe that this strength is inherent in every one of us.

Just as it is important to pay attention to potential health crises or warning signals, it is equally important to find reasons to celebrate the victories.

I eventually threw a party for a small group of her friends and their families that had been in the rehab at the same time Emily had. There were parents, friends, and girlfriends all gathered at our apartment. It was great to see everyone and learn about everything that was happening in their lives.

Maybe it goes without saying that their lives had changed, but it was exciting to hear how much each parent's life had progressed and how a new purpose had been discovered. We all agreed on one thing: there was never really any time to feel down or sorry about what had happened, as each day was filled with tasks and challenges to help our loved ones get accustomed to their new lives. Everyone was still trying to put his or her life back together, and that requires time. As we discussed all that we had been through, I felt a bond with everyone, something I never before would have expected. Through these individuals and family members, I saw that there was indeed life after a traumatic accident, a wonderful life, in fact. These were the original members of the club we had joined, and it was giving each of us more and more confidence in our altered lives with new purpose.

Later that night, as I helped Emily into bed, I told her how proud I was of her. She looked at me with her eyes wide and said, "Thank you, Daddy." It was a simple, but meaningful acknowledgment of all we had been through. Then it was off to the land of dreams where the injury was no longer a factor. Sleep was always a safe place for her. Maybe it took away the reality of being paralyzed. I could only hope this was the case.

Recovery Recap:

—Be patient with recovery

—Accept new challenges while remaining positive

—Pay attention to potential health crises or warning signals

—Find reasons to celebrate

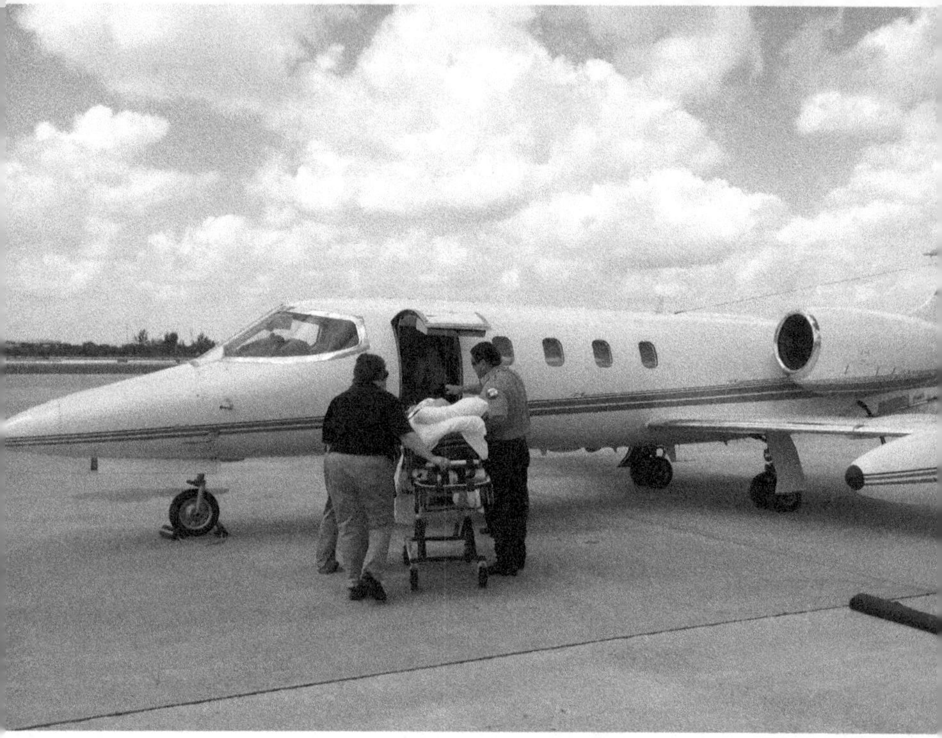

Air Ambulance to Rehab in Michigan

Thrilled to be in 1st Class

CHAPTER 6

ONTO THE INPATIENT REHAB HUNT

You don't have much choice about which trauma center your loved one is sent to; you just go with the flow so that he or she can be stabilized as quickly as possible. However, after your loved one is stabilized and ready for transfer, onward to inpatient rehabilitation you go. Once you are made aware of the diagnoses and have some timeline for discharge, it's time to research the rehabilitation facility that best aligns with the patient's needs.

In some cases, you may only have only a few weeks to find a place. In my case, I had six weeks to perform the research, and even that did not seem like enough time.

I thought the hospital would be very involved in the transitional period between stabilizing Emily's vitals to her entering a rehabilitation facility. The truth is, there are no clear-cut paths or answers. The transition is *"Watch me, learn, and now do it yourself."* There is no real structure that I could rely on.

All I wanted was for someone to say, "Listen, Jack, here's exactly what you do. Here is the facility you will move to next, here are the therapists you'll work with, and here's a manual for all of the procedures you'll need to perform at home."

This simply does not happen. Or at least, it didn't then. Every injury is unique, and therefore, certain inpatient rehabilitation centers may work better for some patients than others.

I was ready to start my evaluation process to find the best place for my daughter right away. I ended up selecting four facilities: Shepherd in Atlanta, Craig in Denver, Jackson Memorial in Miami, and the University of Michigan Health System in Ann Arbor. I traveled to each one and toured the facility to understand more about them.

Admission Criteria

It took a lot of research to determine which one was best for my daughter, and I decided to use that research to create a set of criteria to assist others in rating facilities and making a final decision. Below are those guidelines to help you find the best rehabilitation facility for your loved one.

Ranking

How does the center rate compared with other facilities in the country? Of course, ranking isn't the be-all and end-all measure, but if a facility has a reputation for simply pushing patients through the system, then you probably wouldn't want to send your loved one there. At the very least, you would want to know that ahead of time so you're aware of what you're getting yourself into.

At the time of my research, there were fourteen Spinal Cord Injury Model Systems (SCIMS) across the country. Each center is rated based on certain parameters. I found this extremely helpful in understanding how they performed in regard to their patients.

I asked each facility how patients progressed after leaving the program and whether any case studies were available. I also asked how each compared with other facilities. Patient outcome is a good way of gauging how successful your loved one might be at that particular location. The National Spinal Cord Research Statistical Center (https://www.nscisc.uab.edu) can assist you in learning more about the facility. Each model center is rated against one another, so ask if you can learn more about how the facilities performed.

Program Philosophy

Program philosophy really means, "How does the center run its program?" Staff must have positive methods of treatment and outlook in providing care to their patients. They should be empathetic and realistic, without being too harsh about the reality of the patient's condition. This is an area you should investigate when you visit each facility. Ask questions of the nurses and therapists to get a better understanding and vibe of the facility.

I found that some inpatient rehab programs are more aggressive than others. The typical duration for a spinal cord injury rehab stay is sixty days, but some offer additional time for independent-living coaching. Most facilities offer outpatient programs for additional physical and occupational therapy, to help the patient gain additional functionalities.

Another facility takes a gentler approach with a one-week evaluation, followed by setting functional goals for the patient and working from there. I wanted my daughter to progress at the pace she needed, so we opted for a two-month program in which the facilitators were patient and understanding.

State Funding or Assistance

Is the facility state subsidized? If so, there might be more options in terms of finances, or it could be more limiting. For instance, if you are on Medicaid, then you may be restricted to your state of residence.

One option that does exist when insurance is unavailable is private pay. This can be cost prohibitive, as the majority of programs are "inpatient," whereby the patient is in the facility from sixty to ninety days. But again, the facility may be willing to make a special arrangement on your behalf. You'll never know unless you ask. Your options may seem limited, but before writing off any facilities that you may be interested in, contact those in charge. State your case and see how they might work with you. Options are not always so black-and-white.

Be sure to check both inpatient and outpatient plan coverage with your insurance provider so you understand what charges you may be responsible for. If you don't ask, you won't know.

Location/Community Support

How far away is the center from your home base? Will you be able to commute? Will you be able to temporarily relocate? If a center offers a specific program, it may be worth it to travel. At the same time, being in a familiar place with friends and family for support facilitates a crucial network that will help your loved one recover more quickly during this trying time.

Some centers work hard to help their patients reintegrate back into independent living. This is really the goal here, to help your loved one take back control over his or her life. The more involved the center is after the program, the better. I was fortunate enough to be able to work with the Ann Arbor Center of Independent Living (AACIL), which greatly helped me in many ways, including finding transportation for my daughter's appointments and both of us participating in support groups.

What do the facilities look like? What about the surroundings? You'd be surprised by how much your surroundings can affect your mood and state of mind. Plus, having some green space nearby will allow you, the caretaker, to take a breather every now and then when you need some time alone. Location, community support, and rating ultimately became our primary reason for choosing this facility.

Education for Patient and Family

At this stage, it might be hard to envision what your life will be like once your loved one is finished with the program and back at home. Most likely, you're going to be responsible for a good deal of care, if not long-term care, then at least temporary care. In any case, it is important to be on the same page and know all of the adaptive skills and exercises the patient learns in rehab.

Ask whether the rehab facility has a formal transition program that gives you and the patient tools to be successful at home from both a safety and functional perspective.

Besides physical therapy and occupational therapy, group therapy and psychological counseling is also imperative, as are family education and psychological assistance so the family can learn to adapt and cope with the changes with their loved one. Not all facilities integrate the family into the recovery plan. I recommend a facility that does.

State-of-the-Art Equipment

State-of-the-art equipment isn't necessarily an indicator of patient success, but with so many groundbreaking therapies and methodologies available, you may want your loved one to be in a place where he or she has access to such services. Check out what the facility has to offer in terms of equipment and resources. Ask whether it has a Lokomat, which is a gait-therapy device on a treadmill with constant audio and visual feedback that helps your loved one gain confidence and strength from walking, or a NuStep, or other specific equipment designed for those with your loved one's injury.

Ask about daily routines and if special equipment is limited for certain types of diagnoses. Because Emily's injury was classified as "complete," the Lokomat was not available for her use due to insurance coverage and criteria.

Demographics and Interest

I thought it was important that Emily be around patients with similar injuries within her age group so she wouldn't feel so alone. This may be a consideration for your loved one as well. Having a community of people that is experiencing similar life-changing events helps the individual cope and adjust to his or her new life. The only way you are going to find this information out is to visit the facility in person.

You need a cohesive team to rehabilitate your loved one; make sure the facility you choose is on your team.

I made an effort to only visit centers that seemed truly interested and had availability for the time frame after Emily's expected discharge from the hospital. Why fight to get into a center that isn't fighting for you? *You need a cohesive team to rehabilitate your loved one; make sure the facility you choose is on your team.*

Additional Outpatient Programs

Some facilities have additional programs to participate in, such as day programs to continue PT and OT on an outpatient basis. If there is the possibility for the patient to regain or improve functionality, then insurance companies may allow for further funding for therapy. The decision to provide more funding comes down to the diagnoses, therapist notes, and patient's progress, along with the patient's health insurance.

Based on health insurance regulations, it is imperative that therapists document progress for therapy to continue. Some insurance companies will assign a defined number of therapy sessions for both inpatient and outpatient services. It is important to understand your insurance coverage up front and to not be afraid to appeal if the company denies services. It is also important to be knowledgeable of the diagnostic codes to be able to talk with the medical care providers to make sure you are eligible for insurance coverage. It is better to know up front than to realize later that therapies that would continue to be beneficial are not covered.

In addition, supplemental programs may be affiliated with the facility that may offer specialized use of advanced equipment such as e-stim, which can stimulate muscle contraction with small electrical currents. You may need to petition insurance companies for approval for many of these specialized programs. It's worth the extra effort; keeping that muscle strength and flexibility intact is the absolute best therapy you can do to help regain functionality in the future.

Tallying It Up

What do you do now that you have some basic guidelines by which to rate rehab facilities?

It's time to tally it all up.

When I was considering the best place for my daughter, I took all the areas above and applied a rating to them, from one to three points (one being the best), which was most important to her and me, and then added them up and chose the lowest number. This happened to be the facility at the University of Michigan Health Center, which was in my hometown. I was very fortunate; the center was located six blocks from where I lived at the time. Of course, it was her ultimate decision to choose where she wanted to go.

My daughter had to commit to living in Michigan for the time being, which was difficult for her, as she would miss all of her friends in Florida. We knew it would take a couple of years to get her back home to Florida, but the opportunity was worth it; with diligently petitioning for her to participate in the program, University of Michigan Health System would sponsor her stay until her Medicaid checks came in. GO BLUE!

While the guidelines I offered are a good foundation, ultimately, your decision is a wager. The good news is that, at each of these facilities, there are highly trained professionals who will help your loved one grow stronger each day. You will meet some truly exceptional staff who have candor and grace that will guide your family through the most difficult obstacles to come, and in return, you will see your loved one push harder than you've ever before imagined. We were fortunate to choose the University of Michigan Health System, and its amazing team prepared us for our next steps.

Believe, hope, pray, and persist, and you will be amazed.

Believe, hope, pray, and persist, and you will be amazed.

Recovery Recap:

Inpatient rehabilitation items to consider:

—Program philosophy

—State funding or assistance

—Location/community support

—Education for patient and family

—State-of-the-art equipment

—Demographics and interest

—Additional outpatient programs

Tally it up!

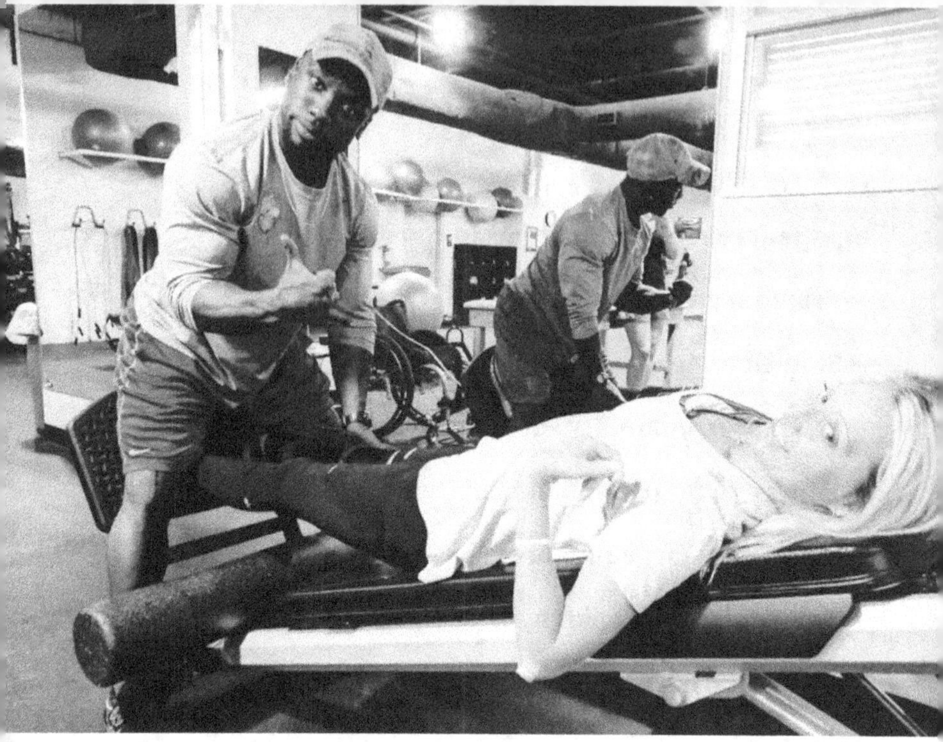

At Barwis Methods with Brian in FL

Rehab at the Recovery Project

At Barwis Methods in MI

CHAPTER 7

GAINING HOPE FROM THE EXPERTS

Winter came, and then the holidays. The good news was that I could spend Christmas at home with Emily and with her sister and family who flew to Michigan for the occasion. We were all happy to be by Emily's side. Along with the usual festivities of holiday visits, it became a family affair to probe every resource available to stay on top of Emily's recovery. We scoured resources to learn more about everything from stem cell research to advanced therapies Emily could be part of to help regain back function in her future.

With the power of the internet, you can spend hours discovering different kinds of research and techniques used for treatments. This proved to be both helpful and frustrating; many of the procedures with the most optimistic results were experimental and therefore not offered in the United States. The United States had taken a long sabbatical from stem cell research, and this put a huge damper on stem cell advancements. Unless we wanted to fly to Europe or South America, we would have to work with more "standard" methods of advanced care in this country.

It was overwhelming to sift through all of the options and to try to make the best decisions possible for Emily's well-being. I wondered whether what I was doing was enough or if there were other stones left unturned.

As if my internal struggle had been sent out into the universe, just before Christmas, I got a surprise call from a person I hadn't heard from in quite some time. She was a member of the condo association I used to belong to and wanted to know if I could help with a particular cause. I started to tell her about my new responsibilities dealing with my daughter's spinal cord injury when she stopped me and urged me to call her husband, Jim. As it turned out, Jim's daughter, Susan, worked in the field of spinal cord injury rehabilitation and headed a research program at a major Southern university.

I called Jim later that night and was surprised by his knowledge about spinal cord injuries. He was curious to learn what kind of injury Emily had and what function she had after the injury, and at the end of the conversation, he offered to arrange a meeting between his daughter and Emily.

Jim shared about his daughter, who speaks internationally regarding new research on spinal cord injury. I was amazed to learn that she was actually one of the doctors who had cared for Christopher Reeves after his injury. She helped Reeves using Locomatt Training, a type of therapy used to help individuals experience walking movement through lower extremity weight bearing. Without movement, your body has a habit of forgetting how to move or perform walking. Many individuals utilize this therapy to prepare their mind and body for the skills needed to walk again.

This chance phone call appeared to be a miracle in disguise.

Everything Jim said filled me with hope, and when I learned that his daughter would be home for Christmas in just a few days, I felt a strong presence within me. I couldn't believe that a major research doctor would be visiting our home to talk to Emily about what she could do to help her. I could hardly wait to tell Emily the exciting news. Someone who had spent her career trying to find answers to assist an individual such as Emily, was actually coming to meet and help her.

Two days after Christmas, we received our belated Christmas present, and what a present it was! As soon as Susan came into our condo, she got down to business. She told us about how the research that she was involved in could change everything for those who had experienced a spinal cord injury.

Research had revealed that the spinal cord has its own kind of memory, she said. And like memory, the spinal cord could be taught to remember. It was a principle she used throughout her work with individuals who had undergone a spinal cord injury, and it had held up in many types of experiments.

After running the gamut of medical questions pertaining to Emily's condition, Susan asked for a small ball. I grabbed a tennis ball and gave it to her. She then passed it to Emily. She showed Emily how to squeeze the ball, while at the same time, thinking about what it feels like.

"Think about the ball, from the soft fuzz to the firmness of the rubber," she instructed. She explained that the mind needs to remember the sensation and the ability to contract muscles in order to squeeze the ball. In essence, Emily needed to teach the spinal cord to remember the feeling of a tennis ball.

Susan walked Emily through the complete experience. You wouldn't think that describing a tennis ball would take long, but they spent a solid ten minutes going through the motions. When Susan finished her tutorial, she handed the ball back to Emily.

"Now do one thousand," Susan said.

Emily looked at her in disbelief.

"One thousand?" she asked. "That will take me all day."

Susan responded, "Well do you have anything else going on right now?"

Touché, I thought. She was measuring Emily up, gauging whether she had the will. Never one to back down from a challenge, Emily got to work. She ultimately did not make it to one thousand, but she impressed Susan with her ability to twitch her forefinger after a valiant effort.

"With the right technique and practice, you will improve and gain more function over time," she encouraged Emily.

I looked at my daughter and saw that the hope I had felt for her had finally caught on. Emily was ready to get to work, and it would take a team composed of people like Susan to help coach Emily through. The team continued to be developed.

Emily would spend hundreds of hours with various therapists and trainers down the line. She continues to work with both therapists and physical trainers to help her maintain and build strength along with stretching muscles to allow better range of motion for years to come. Some of these people have become like family.

Some have helped her reach new heights in her recovery and make gains beyond anything she had thought possible. Others . . . well, I hate to say it, but there have been some people who have hindered the process rather than helped. But both groups of individuals have taught us valuable lessons.

The therapists and trainers will become the closest people in your life. They will witness your ups and downs, learn your vulnerabilities and strengths, and push you when you feel you cannot go any further.

These people are the true superstars and your best assistant coaches.

Finding great therapists and trainers is no easy matter. I found that once I felt comfortable telling friends and acquaintances about my quadriplegic daughter, connections seemed to form. Just as Susan had brought in her expert advice to show Emily and me that there was hope for new developments in functionality, she also introduced us to knowledgeable people. Susan later invited Emily to apply for a two-year program at her medical research center that would implant electrodes around her spinal cord. All Emily needed to do was to pay for room and board and participate in the daily activities. Emily ended up as number nine out of the five selected into the program, but the opportunity was well within her reach.

Shortly after we met Susan on that cold day in December, I received a call from a close dear friend, Sue Ellen. She told me of a trainer, Mike Barwis, who was the strength coach at the University of Michigan but was now working with professional sports athletes, including an individual named Brock Mealer. That name seemed so familiar. Then it came to me. Emily and I had watched him on national TV. He walked out onto the field at a football game the first week she was at inpatient rehab in Michigan. Brock's story is amazing. He had sustained a serious injury and was told that he had less than a 1 percent chance of being able to walk again. When he walked out on the field that day in September of 2010, my daughter looked at me and said, "I want to be like him."

I sent a text to Mike and received a reply back, "Any friend of Sue Ellen is a friend of mine. Bring her in next week, and we will see how we can help her."

And so that's what we did. The "Barwis Method" gym was conveniently located only twenty minutes from our home. The people there were nothing less than fantastic and friendly. Mike was able to find new muscle sensation and activation below Emily's injury level. With hard work, determination, and focus, there was hope that she could regain function.

Emily was matched with ex pro football player Dan Moses as her trainer for close to two years before she moved down to Florida. Even though she is now living in Florida, she still goes to one of the Mike Barwis gyms with the same positive attitude to succeed. Experts with that positive influence will get you where you need to go. As your loved one's caregiver and advocate, you have to be his or her coach, but you must also connect with someone you can learn from and build your team with integrity and quality.

We had the very best coaches available to help Emily gain strength and, down the road, to regain function and more independence. Our team was certainly gaining steam.

Recovery Recap:

—Spread the word about your loved one and build connections

—Utilize all tools you have, word of mouth, recommendations, guides, to find medical help

—Build an all-star team to help your loved one rehabilitate like a champ

Thomas and Ashley with Transfer

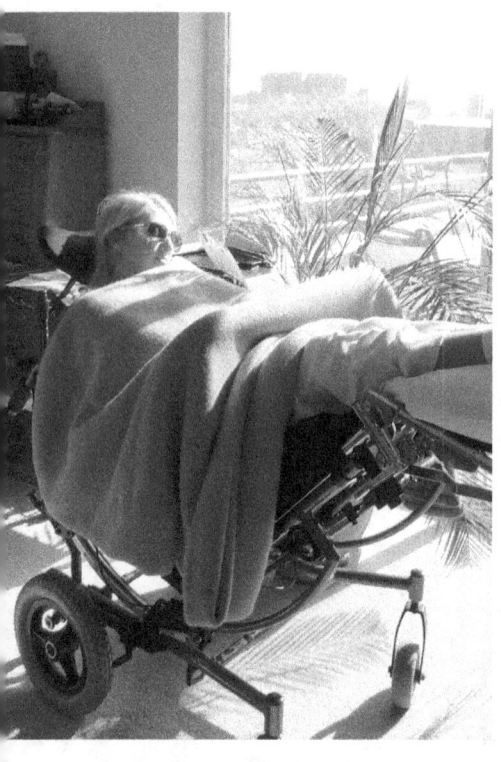

Warming in AA

Sis and Emily

CHAPTER 8

ADVOCATING AND GETTING THE MOST FROM DOCTORS AND NURSES

I learned all about daily operations while Emily was in the ICU, seeing as I was there more than twelve hours a day. I was amazed by how the hospital staffed and organized each unit of the building. The goal always seemed to be to maintain quality and safety, along with consistency of care, not an easy task, to say the least.

When you are the parent of a child in the ICU, you pay attention to every detail, including how long it takes to see the nurse after you push the call button. As I was a concerned father who was new to the patient-advocate role, you can imagine just how often that button was pushed. I was one of those annoying parents who asked question after question. Each day, there was a doctor overseeing Emily's care, so that was the person I wanted to be sure to talk to when he or she made their rounds.

My success in actually connecting with the doctor was another story. I understand the hospital is busy and that some patients take longer than others, so for the staff, it would be impossible to schedule a particular time with a patient let alone an bothersome parent. That means you have to learn the patterns and let it be known to each nurse that you want to see the doctor when he or she comes around.

Once I became familiar with the doctor's and nurse's schedule and routine, I was sure to be prepared ahead of time with all my pertinent questions. Most of my questions were about Emily's status, whether or not there was anything to concern me or if there were any changes to the course of action. I wanted to know that everyone was on the same page with her recovery; talking to the on-call doctor was a start.

The nurses hold an important part of the puzzle, and in some cases, more than the doctors, as they are in the trenches with the patient every day. The best way to get information is to build a relationship in a nonthreatening way. I was only after information, not to question a course of action or tell the staff what I thought they were doing wrong.

In a few cases, I ruffled some feathers, which is to be expected. Some nurses and doctors will give you the dumbed-down version of what they think you should know, but that wasn't going to cut it for me. As an advocate for Emily, I needed facts, and if I could not spell it or pronounce it, I had to write it down and then research it.

When I had first become a health care advocate for my father, who was having all kinds of health issues including dementia, depression and other neurological disease, I learned early on to be diplomatic with my inquiries and not to create conflict, which can happen when staff is busy dealing with other people's lives. I did not want to get in the way of my daughter's recovery, but I had to make it clear what my expectations were as her advocate. When it came down to it, my only purpose was to understand my daughter's condition and make informed decisions in the best interest of her health.

In the world of health care, a health-care advocate assists, coordinates, collaborates, co-manages, identifies, educates, and provides services to the patient, or in my case, my daughter. This is one of the most important roles you will have if you decide to take on the mission. It is a mission of great importance, and you will need to be assertive but diplomatic with the medical staff.

As the advocate, you will assist your loved one in navigating the health-care system to address any health-care needs. You will comanage his or her health care by removing obstacles, providing timely access to care, delivering personalized care, and promoting safe and quality outcomes. Be sure to remember, however, that you will not be working alone in your quest. Your ability to communicate and develop relationships in the medical community is very important.

The feats doctors and nurses perform may seem amazing, but doctors and nurses are indeed still people. And like all people, they vary in terms of their ability to communicate, their temperament, and their work style. Balancing these relationships requires some skill. Here are some tips to do just that:

Know Your Audience

You must be able to communicate with whoever is providing your loved one with care. As his or her advocate, you want to know every single thing going on with his or her recovery. You also want to be sure that each person who comes in to help your loved one is in the loop and on board with the medical plan and your role as advocate.

This is where any innate talent for conversation comes in handy, not just small talk, but also the ability to talk to anybody and relate to him or her on some level. The only way you can communicate effectively is understand who you are talking with first and be a good listener.

Questions Show that You Care

It makes all the difference to simply talk to your loved one's health-care providers. Being present and asking questions shows that you care. When I was engaged and asking questions, they knew that I was on top of things, which provides more accountability across the board. Of course, asking questions required me to do some research first.

This, again, relies on good communication and respect. No one is perfect. If individuals know you're not threatening or challenging them, then they will be more open to collaborate with you.

Cross-Check Health Care Providers So Everyone Is on the Same Page

You're dealing with a lot of personalities in medical facilities. Nurses work twelve hours a day, three shifts a week, and sometimes overtime. The hospital may run two shifts a day, and if you catch a nurse at the end of that twelve-hour shift, more likely than not, he or she will be flat-out exhausted. Even when beginning a shift, the nurse may not be totally up to date on what happened during the last shift.

If you do the math, this means you may have different nurses and CNAs throughout the week, not considering others, or floaters, who may come in during a shift. In addition, there will be multiple doctors on call, and this makes it more difficult for consistency of care, let alone, for you to get dependable answers.

Separate nurses and CNAs will be caring for your loved one during the day, and another set at night puts the focus on two things: continuity and consistency of care.

Our hope is that continuation of care and consistency will continue no matter who is working; however, that is not always the case. You may need to become a conduit for information. If you hear something that does not make sense from another care provider, be sure to voice your concern.

Treat Staff with Respect

Doctors and nurses are also the ones who will help you prepare for the big transition back home. Many of the things they do, you will soon have to do at home. So you'll need to work with them to learn how things are done. So much in life is just about knowing how to work with other people. Once your loved one is stable and you have determined which rehabilitation center he or she will move to, the recovery process becomes its own small entity. You have a team of medical professionals managing all aspects of recovery that need attention to each area of care. In many ways, it's like a small organization, and it deserves the attention to detail and accountability of any serious enterprise. By ensuring the people who provide the care and rehab for your loved one are all on the same page, you will ignite the inherent power of people who are all working together to help your loved one heal and grow.

Recovery Recap:

—Know your audience

—Questions show that you care

—Cross-check health providers

—Treat medical care providers with respect

Ride to Zingermans

First Night Out Since Accident

UM Football Coach Richrod with Emi

CHAPTER 9

GOING PUBLIC

If there's one thing I learned throughout my journey with Emily, it's that life has a way of balancing out. For every loss, there is a gain; for every sorrow, there will be joy. And for every item that is missed from previous experiences, there are new opportunities to be treasured. A traumatic event is like a splash in the water; when it first erupts, you can't see past the chaos, but eventually the water becomes smooth and returns to calm.

This lesson was learned not in therapy or in the hospital; rather, it was learned in the discussions with my daughter that followed her return home. I found myself looking through Emily's eyes and discovering strength and resilience I had never known. It was like I was getting to know her all over again. And while much of it was enlightening, there were some difficult moments, too.

As we grew accustomed to our routine, we began to open up. No longer did we need to focus on the present and all of its demands. Finally, there was room for reflection.

In the morning, I was her caretaker; in the afternoon, I was her coach. But in the evening, I was just her father and friend. And on a few evenings, the discussion would turn to the night of the accident.

These conversations were extremely difficult to have, but I understood how important it was for Emily to address the circumstances surrounding the night her life dramatically changed.

She never did remember anything about the accident that day. All memory was lost. The hardest part for her was making sense of why the accident happened.

Emily typically did not cry, but when we spoke of the day that changed her life, inevitably tears would flow on both sides. The hardest part of these conversations was waiting until I was alone to sob and release my own sadness. Although I spent every day with her, I couldn't—and still can't—imagine what it must be like for such a beautiful young woman to realize she was paralyzed from the chest down.

There were many equally trying topics that plagued Emily. Time passed, and she gained perspective, which inevitably brought questions, questions that had no answers. Her hardest question was whether anyone would ever love her now that she was disabled. At these moments, she felt as if she were no longer a whole person. Emily wondered how someone could love someone who was "less than others."

This was one myth I had no problem dispelling. She was in no way "less than." In fact, she was "more than." She had grown to be more compassionate, more grateful, and more loving. And for most of us, those are the qualities that really matter.

"There will be men in your life, when you are ready," I said. "Do not accept any pity or sympathy. You are much more than what you think."

When I looked at her, I saw someone I never knew before the accident: a strong woman, resilient and wise from experience. I knew she would one day have a relationship with a special person, but I also knew that she would have to become more independent in order to function more on her own, or with another person.

Another difficult subject was the question of whether she would be able to have a family one day. It broke my heart when she confided in me her sadness.

"I'll never have babies," she said. "I'll never be able to take care of them or even feel them touch me." When she said this, I couldn't hold back the tears. Thinking of how much my children had meant to me, and how much I wished for my own children to experience having children, left me speechless. I never knew how to respond. All I did know was that there was no reason to rule out any of her dreams.

"You will have children some day," I encouraged her. "With the right person. It just might be a little more complicated for you. Today it may seem out of reach, but tomorrow it will be well within."

She would talk about the physical setbacks of her injury. How she would have to rely on someone for the rest of her life, how sitting in a chair was uncomfortable, not just physically, but also in terms of the stares she would get. Part of her wanted the people who stared to look past her, but part of her also wanted them to pay attention.

I'd try to remind her that after the accident, there were more opportunities for her than before, opportunities to help others and to have an impact on the world. Even though her mobility had changed, her ability to be successful had only grown.

She wanted to be able to run again, as she did back in Florida to stay in shape. Yoga was yet another activity that she loved (although I'll never understand her favorite, "hot yoga," which is basically sweating out toxins with the temperature above one hundred degrees).

Some things she would be able to do sooner than others. She wanted to drive again, something she would do once she got her new license and a vehicle fitted to her new abilities. The only problem there was that she wanted a Jeep and not the "soccer mom" minivan that was the typical for families. I reassured her that there would be other options, including autonomous cars that drive themselves. She agreed that they are right around the corner; however, she reminded me that driving is the ultimate independence. She wanted freedom from the new normal she was experiencing, and who could blame her for not wanting this independence?

These types of conversations did not happen every night, but when they did, it was exhausting for both of us. Sometimes, she would always end up wishing to go back to what her life was before the accident, a hopeless feeling. As a parent, you can do little. After all, you can't change the reality of the situation, and sometimes it's just as impossible to change a loved one's mind-set. Sometimes, the best thing you can do is to just be there for him or her and listen.

On nights such as these, I would just give her a hug and sit beside her bed until she fell asleep. She was going through the grieving process, and it would be some time before the waves of sorrow lessened to tides and then ripples.

These conversations brought me out of my rooted existence in the present and got me thinking about the future. We had goals for Emily ever since the day she had pulled through after the accident. But now it was time to go beyond the hospital and beyond the home that had become her safety net.

It was time to get back to real life, one step at a time.

Back at inpatient rehab, Emily had a wonderful recreation therapist named Devin. He was skilled at what he did, not just because he had good training, but also because he had a knack for connecting with Emily and putting her at ease. In my mind, there was no better person to help us achieve Emily's first big step, which was leaving the inpatient rehab to go out to a restaurant in public.

I chose a restaurant that I knew specifically because it employed disabled individuals, had great customer service, and it served organic food of the best quality. When I called to make the reservation, I explained how important this was for Emily, having her first outing since her accident. I wanted to be sure it was a stress-free and positive experience.

Part of me was worried. I felt that if it were up to Emily, she would just stay in. I braced myself for a big pep talk leading up to the night, but Emily surprised me by her eagerness to go. I realized she was putting on a brave face because she knew how much I wanted this for her.

Devin drove the hospital van out to the restaurant. Once we arrived, it took some time to get her out of the van with her power chair and even more time to navigate it through the restaurant. Inside, we were taken to a half booth with two chairs on the opposite side.

That's when the first mini-crisis arose: Emily tried to get herself under the table, but it was too low. The power chair could barely get within range of the table. We asked for another table that would work, but there was no such luck. All the tables were too low, so we just had to make do.

I was hoping something like this would not happen, but it proved to be a good trial run. Inevitably, there would be more situations like this in the future. There would be awkward times when she would need to adapt. This just happened to be the first one. While initially it was embarrassing for her, in the end, she realized it was no big deal.

The appetizers came, and then the entrées. We were having a good, relaxing time until Devin stopped to scold me.

I had been helping Emily eat and not letting her do it herself. Emily had to do it on her own, no matter how long it took. It was to teach her that she needed to order food that she could eat without help. This was all about helping Emily learn how to be independent out in the real world. There would be times that I would not be with her, so she needed to know what she could and could not do.

This was not just a social event, but also one to learn from, to explore ways to work around the deficiencies of access in public places. Soon there would be another opportunity to do just that.

The second event we went to was a tailgate party for all the patients and their family members, including the medical staff from the rehabilitation wing. Prior to the event, I was messaging back and forth with my good hiking friend, Wendi. I updated her on all that was going on and told her about the tailgate party we were going to in a few days at Michigan Stadium. She then asked me if Emily would like to meet the University of Michigan head football coach. I replied back in seconds, "Absolutely." Within forty-eight hours, it was all set up, and to our surprise, it would happen at the tailgate party with all the staff and her new friends and family there.

Coach Rich Rodriguez walked into the outdoor area where we were all gathered, came up to us immediately, and introduced himself to Emily. His first question was whether she liked football. She nodded her head, and soon they were talking about all sorts of things. Finally, she decided to introduce me, and as I shook his hand, he took his other hand from behind his back and pulled out a signed football that said, "To Team Emily. Keep fighting and don't give up! We are pulling for you! All the best! Go Blue!"

This was nothing short of a major success for Emily. She continued to talk with the coach without being in any way nervous.

At one point, he looked up at me and said, "Whenever you would like to take your beautiful daughter to a football game, you let me know." I was in complete awe with his kindness.

Many of the staff could not believe that he had made that appearance. In fact, when he was asked what had brought him there that day, he looked at Emily and said, "This is the reason I am here, to present this football to Emily." He continued to be bombarded with people, but kept coming back to Emily and telling her that he was there for her. He made the day unforgettable. What an inspiration he was!

When I looked at Emily that night, she had a glow about her. Her life wasn't about hospitals and diagnoses and treatments; for that day, it was about being recognized by a Big Ten football coach. I knew we were in the right place. I couldn't wait to see what next to come. *Just another one of God's blessing when her world seemed so overwhelming.*

Times will be trying, emotional, and upsetting, but your loved one is learning to cope with her new life. It can take up to five years or longer for her to adjust and accept her new situation. Allow her to adjust to being out in public and help her establish good communication skills.

Recovery Recap:

—Keep an open ear and an open mind.

—When first "going public," take things slowly.

—Research venues ahead of time

—Don't stress about it

—Learn from each experience and make adjustments

—Encourage your loved one to be vocal and clear about his or her needs

Dinner with Dad and Sis

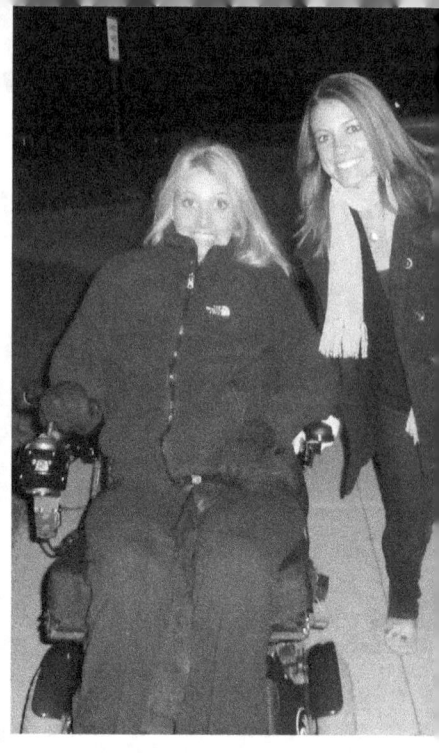

Michigan in the Winter

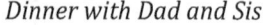

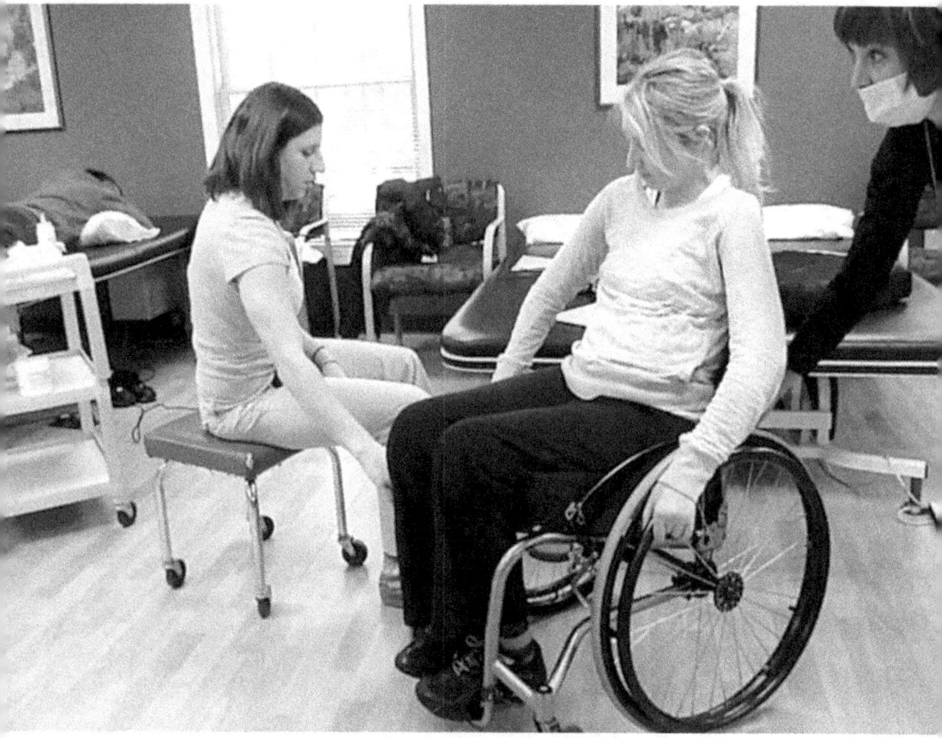

Rehab with New Chair

CHAPTER 10

FLYING THE REHAB COOP

After Emily spent so much time in the hospital and rehab facility, no one was happier to be back home than she was. Yet the move was bittersweet; instead of going back to her life in Florida, she was coming to stay temporarily with me.

Over the next two years, Emily would use that vision of the Florida coast to drive her to become strong enough to live on her own. Watching her determination, I knew that if she set her sights on it, she would achieve it, but in the meantime, we had to get used to sharing the condo in downtown Ann Arbor. Not only did I have to share with her, but also we had to open up the home to caregivers who would be helping her when I eventually went back to work. This was very difficult because I was used to keeping a clean and organized home. Once I opened up my residence, it would never be the same.

For a quadriplegic and an adult child, moving home is a larger matter than simply unpacking the suitcase and settling in. A person who is in a wheelchair requires certain adaptations and equipment inside the home to live safely and more efficiently. When I first looked into the various needs Emily would have at home, I was overwhelmed by the amount of equipment, adaptive technologies, and applications to help quadriplegics, and so I decided to wait until Emily was officially back to see what we actually needed.

When she first came back from the hospital, the plan was to stay at the condo temporarily until we could figure out a better housing situation that allowed for the adaptations Emily needed. The condo was on the seventh floor and was actually quite nice because it had plenty natural light, was on one floor, and was very open. I was originally only going to stay for a year to try out Ann Arbor city living, but that changed when it became critical to have a suitable living situation on one floor with wheelchair access. I was very fortunate that I had that going for me.

As part of the rehab process, when it was time to go home, the facility would assess the condo to be sure it was safe for Emily. The only change we had to make to the condo was purchasing a shower chair designed to fit to the bathtub with the ability to tilt back. The power chair that Emily needed for mobility provided pressure relief so she would be less apt to get pressure sores; the only problem was that the chair itself was a beast.

The elevator in the condo was a bonus, along with not having any steps up to the complex. But what would we do if the elevator were out of service? There were a few times when Emily was up in the condo alone while the elevator was stuck. We made it through, but it was frustrating nonetheless.

The firefighters and police had my daughter's information in case there was an emergency or issue, including if the elevator was not functioning. This seemed to be standard for a paralyzed individual in any city and certainly very comforting to me. Make sure that you contact the fire and police station in your area.

Adapting at Home

I learned so much about adapting the home and equipment to support the needs of a quadriplegic after a major accident. When you move back home, there will be certain learning curves you have to overcome. First and foremost, realize that it takes time. Everything you're used to doing in a certain time, multiply that by three. Because that's how long it will take you to do it now.

Time was a tough obstacle that made it extremely challenging to get to morning appointments. It would take three to four hours to go through her entire morning routine each day. There were some caregivers who were so efficient that they could do it in less than two hours every time, but every person is different, so we had to always plan for the maximum time.

Pertinent to time is routine. Routine will allow you to manage the time and tasks you have. By creating a routine for all of the medications, stretching, exercises, and daily programs, you are saving your sanity and your loved one's well-being.

We chose to post a daily schedule that could be followed by all the different caregivers who would come to the house, including when I was in the rotation. With rotation comes variance, especially when you have yet again different individuals performing the activities. In these moments of "variance," remember that you are only human and are doing your best. No need to stress over running late, for it's part of the deal (and with my daughter, it was more the rule than the exception).

New Equipment

Emily came home in a power chair that had amazing torque and the ability to tilt her back to relieve pressure from her butt. The chair was very bulky and awkward. The size and weight of the power chair made it difficult to fit it in the car; however, Ann Arbor is one of the most "access friendly" cities in America. For only five dollars, we could arrange any ride to an appointment as long as it was in the city. (If we had to go outside the city, then the costs jumped from five to seventy-five dollars, as that would require private transport.) We eventually purchased our own van for more flexibility, but the city's service was a great help in the months prior.

The van we decided upon was a used 2007 Dodge Caravan with a motorized ramp and quick-lock system for ease of securing the chair to the vehicle. It was used, of course; we had no need to buy something new until we knew more about how she would get around and what type of wheelchair she would be using. This quickly proved to be a challenge.

When Emily was in rehab, the physical therapist never did give her a choice of what type of chair Emily would like. The therapist just assumed that the power chair was what her diagnoses level needed in order to be safe and mobile, and so that's what Emily received.

Emily quickly found the power chair to be very limiting in terms of her movement in stores and restaurants. Any steps, even some thresholds in doorways, were impassable, and in most cases, the chair would not fit under a standard table.

It was also a behemoth piece of equipment. The chair weighed close to three hundred pounds.

I had wished that we had been informed more about wheelchairs in the beginning because her mobility in social settings was more important than the ability to operate the chair with no assistance. This became a real issue for her and would need to be addressed so that she could feel more comfortable being out in public.

The time came when we decided to change out the chairs. Emily started looking at manual chairs with power-assist wheels that would make the wheels very easy to maneuver. Emily chose a company called TiLite. She had a new friend who was going to the Recovery Project and who was very influential, so Emily was adamant about picking this manufacturer. Emily learned from therapy about a rehab hospital that would do a fitting for ninety-nine dollars as long as the patient ordered the chair from the company that is associated with this hospital. We made an appointment and paid the money up front.

At the appointment, the representative took an astounding number of measurements and talked about fit and pressure sores and everything else under the sun. This seemed to be the best of the best in terms of manual chairs. Emily decided on wheels that would power assist, requiring less effort in getting the chair moving. They could be programmed in many different ways, and for the cost, they should be. The wheels alone were seven thousand dollars!

After spending four hours there, we left feeling confident that the chair would not only look good, but also, it would fit her needs.

Once I signed off on the chair, it started being built. The chair took more than six weeks to build, and then scheduling delivery took even longer. After almost three months of waiting, we finally heard back that we needed a final fitting and that someone would deliver it to the hospital.

And when I first saw her in her new set of wheels, I forgot all about the trouble and headaches leading up to its arrival. Emily looked so happy that I couldn't help but snap a few pictures.

The charm did not last long. After we realized it was the wrong fit for Emily, I knew we would have to once again begin the laborious process of finding another wheelchair. The chair did not have enough "dump," and for her, that was critical, especially because she was a new quadriplegic. Dump is needed for the individual to stay in the chair without falling forward, as she has no core strength to keep herself upright.

I contacted both the company servicing the chair and the person who had fitted her in it, along with the head customer-service rep for the manufacturer. I also called our new friend who happened to represent TiLite. He was able to pull strings and bring some attention to our case. He told me that the rep was going to be in town the next week, along with the district manager, and both wanted to meet us because we had such a poor experience with our recent purchase.

When we finally got together, we worked out a deal that would give Emily a new, correctly sized chair with a substantial discount. She would be able to keep her current chair, which would give her a backup. I had hoped that this chair would see her back to Florida.

The lesson learned is to always do your research up front. Even when the experts in the industry are telling you something you need, you should always ask questions and take time to research their recommendations. For Emily, it was about being in a smaller manual chair from day one. You can only make the best decisions possible with the information you have at the time; however, there can be better options out there.

Being Comfortable at Home

Once you are home, you will quickly learn what you need. Although there is a lot of technology out there to make your home more accessible, you will also learn to adapt. You won't be able to purchase every adaptation you need, so you have to come up with your own solutions that make sense. Buying everything is not the answer and the cost can be outrageous. Usually you can find solutions that are more practical for adaptation. One is able to understand what is needed better than suppliers, manufacturers, and sometimes, what the therapists are able to suggest..

Prior to Emily's moving in with me, I decided that a hospital bed would make it easier to help her transfer. I wanted the bed to have the ability to be raised and lowered, including the head and feet. Also important to me were rails to hold her in from falling out just in case her legs had a spasm that generated some movement. Then there was the risk of pressure sorcs, so a special mattress was also high on the list of priorities.

I ended up writing to the CEO of a major hospital bed manufacturer, asking if there were any programs that would allow the rental or donation of a bed with those desired features.

I received a letter back from the CEO's assistant indicating the company would put me in contact with a foundational group. Within just a few weeks, in time for Emily, when she came home, an amazing new hospital bed was delivered with all the bells and whistles needed. This proved to be one of the most valued pieces of equipment for all of us.

There's a lot of technology out there. You can control lights, appliances, and the thermostat, but they must be installed and configured to use. There is so much available, but is it really necessary, and will it actually provide comfort?

One of the most important pieces of technology was a communication device. Emily had an iPhone, and with the small investment of twenty-five dollars, we purchased a loop that would attach to the back of the phone so she could hold it. It turns out that her phone became the center of performing everything from turning off lights to opening the door to adjusting the thermostat (as long as wireless devices were utilized).

Before taking the plunge, wait to see what you actually need. Usually, the person can find ways to adapt, given the time to try things out. There are certain things I found I had to buy, and there are certain changes I had to make to the home. I had to buy a commode/shower chair to fit in the bathtub, along with a Hoyer Lift to get Emily in and out of her wheelchair, bed, and shower chair. The shower chair tilted back to help moderate Emily's blood pressure while she was in the bathroom.

Door openings have to be a minimum of thirty inches wide, or wider, if you're going to use a power chair. Therefore, I had a few thresholds that needed to be addressed. This required purchasing a couple of thresholds ramps to allow her to roll over.

Most of these items will be unbelievably expensive, but if you take time to really figure out what you need, you will save yourself a lot of money and time. If something is outside the reach of your budget, look to manufacturers to see if there are any discounts, programs or grants that will help you pay for the equipment. Don't be afraid to ask.

Wait and do little things, one at a time. The most important thing is to be able to get your loved one in and out of the rooms of the house, especially the bedroom and bathroom.

Having adaptive spoons, forks, and silverware for someone who doesn't have fine motor skills is a good investment. But waiting and trying things out makes far better sense than buying into all of the technology that will be pitched your way. Many therapists and manufacture reps will be pushing you into purchasing, but in most cases, it is much better to wait and determine what your most important needs are once you are at home.

As time goes on, you may find you need even less technology. In the first two months, Emily went from a power chair to a manual chair, which was a huge transition. She also learned how to do some tasks without the assistance of adaptive devices. She wanted to be able to adapt without modified adaptive equipment, and that continues to be her main goal today. Every year was like a step down from the amount of help and equipment she needed the year before.

I'll never forget the doom and gloom I felt when a rehab doctor told us in Florida, "You'd better prepare yourself to spend a quarter million on all the things she's going to need. She'll need a power chair with full capabilities and tons of technology in the home to function. She'll need all kinds of things."

I found that he was completely wrong. My total investment in the first year, including an accessible van with a ramp, was less than twenty-five thousand dollars.

When you get home, your loved one will not be doing what they were doing two years ago, nor will they be in the same position two years from now. They will further adapt and they will find better ways to get everyday tasks done.

Recovery Recap:

—Allow more time for everyday tasks

—Build a routine

—Research transportation options in your hometown

—Remember that adaptation is trial by error

—Before buying equipment, wait to see what you will actually need

—Allow your loved one to seek and find adaptive solutions

Getting Ready to Hit the Town in AA

Sally, Don, Dad, Emily, and Polly at Benefit

CHAPTER 11

CARING FOR YOURSELF WHILE YOU'RE CARING FOR ANOTHER

If you've had a child, then maybe you can remember the early days, the days when you couldn't eat a meal without interruption, relax with a book, or even sleep through the night. It's as if, all of a sudden, hours disappeared from the day. There's not even time to wonder where the time went, because you have a hundred other things to keep track of.

Being a new parent brings about a certain kind of stress caused by realizing that suddenly, you have another person's life in your hands. It is up to you to care for him or her and raise him or her into adulthood. At first, this stress will keep you up at night until you are able to adapt, which takes time. . With time, you start to get the hang of the whole parenting thing.

The best gift you could give your children is to teach them how to care for themselves because you won't always be around to do it for them. This is where being a great coach comes as a priority.

Rule number one for any caregiver is to take care of yourself first. In many ways, caring for a loved one after a catastrophic injury is like tending to your first baby. You feel as if his or her health and happiness are in your hands, and indeed, it is all you can think about. Many of the same feelings and stressors arise. You forget about sleep, forget about your social life, forget about everything except for caring for this important person.

The best gift you could give your children is to teach them how to care for themselves because you won't always be around to do it for them. This is where being a great coach comes as a priority.

Eventually, this cycle of constant attention will cause burn out. You simply can't keep going, going, going without stopping every now and then to take care of yourself. People who are exhausted and stressed out are more likely to have a reduced immune system, making them more susceptible to sickness and disease. It can also cause bad decisions to be made or frustrations to be taken out in the wrong direction.

Your loved one's life has changed, and now he or she is learning to adapt to this new reality. When you are a parent and caregiver, your attention is so focused on that goal that it's easy to forget that your life has changed too. And you have to learn how to take care of yourself all over again. The more you keep your own well-being in balance, the more you will enhance your coping skills, increase your stamina and stay healthy.

Your relationships might be changing. Your ability to work is stretched thin. Perhaps your own health is being compromised because you've put it on the back burner. It is easy to neglect yourself when someone you love is in need.

You are an important part of his or her recovery process. By learning to manage your life outside of the hospital, rehab process, and the caregiving, you are also succeeding in being the best support possible for your loved one.

Communicate with Your Employer

First and foremost, you have to protect your livelihood. When a crisis emerges, you have to make arrangements with your employer to keep your affairs in order.

I'm the boss at work, and perhaps was too involved in the day-to-day activities, which made it harder to be away. I was worried about how the business might continue in my absence, but after I sent an email to alert my employees of the situation, they all stepped up and took care of business. I was fortunate to have a team that wanted to help, but I needed to ask first.

Conversely, if you work for a company, then it is crucial that you talk to your employer. Being absent from work is a scary thing; you wonder if you can keep your job, if you'll be able to get the time you need to help your loved one, and how this will change your relationship with your employer. Don't be afraid to be honest about your situation. You may qualify for the Federal Family and Medical Leave Act (FMLA). This would give you up to twelve weeks of unpaid time during the year. Stick to the facts and be clear on what you need, the sooner, the better.

Enlist a Friend or Family Member to Help Manage Your Affairs

Whether you are across the country or across town, you will be spending a lot of time at the health-care facility. Chances are that it will be difficult to stay on top of household chores, such as paying the bills and responding to important notices. You've got enough on your mind; enlist a friend to help manage your affairs at home so nothing slips through the cracks. I did this by redirecting mail to a friend who monitored it for any critical items. Staying on top of your bills will alleviate additional stress when you finally do return home.

Take a Break

After the accident, I received weekly updates from my team at work, but they were delayed and small in nature. They hid issues so I could focus on helping my daughter. The intention was to make life easier for me, but in truth, it only made it more stressful when I finally did return to work. Essentially, the business lost focus because I had been away for too long. Even though I appreciated my employees' help and support, my leave affected the bigger picture, which ended up adding more stress to my life.

Emily's mother was also steadfast at the hospital. It was too difficult for us to even think of going away. It got to the point where we all needed a break from the madness.

I realized I had to leave, not just to check in at work but also to check in with myself. I finally scheduled a flight back to Michigan for four days to manage some business and to participate in a personal commitment I had made to the Leukemia & Lymphoma Society (LLS). This was a hiking commitment to raise funds for LLS. It was extremely difficult to leave my daughter. I explained that I needed to take care of a few things at home and for myself and asked if she was okay with that. She looked straight into my eyes and nodded. I could sense that she really didn't want me to go, but she understood I needed to go for my own good and hers too. I felt she was in great hands, and I could always fly down at a moment's notice if there were an issue.

The flight home allowed me to clear my mind for a little while. I was overwhelmed by everything going on in my life. My parents were also living in Florida, and my father's health had been deteriorating prior to the accident. I had recently stepped up to care for them. It was nice to be in a quiet space for a few hours, but the reprieve did not last long; soon enough, I had hit the ground running.

My trip was a success. I touched base with work and would be working on a few things back in Florida. I also met with the Social Security Administration to start Emily's disability and apply for Medicare, and I had a couple of days in the mountains hiking with a great group of LLS survivors, families that had lost loved ones, and those who had other connections to the disease. I felt more relaxed and more in balance with myself; however, I knew it would not be for long.

I felt anxious driving back to the airport for my return flight. I was eager to see Emily but nervous about all that lay ahead. On the plane, I once again felt a sense of peace. It only lasted a few minutes before an older gentleman sat down next to me and asked my reason for being in Florida. Clearly, he did not know what he was getting himself into.

I told him about my daughter, and to my surprise, he was a very compassionate listener and wanted to know more about what had happened. An hour went by, and the subject turned to fishing.

"Ah," the man said. "I've got something for you." He reached into his briefcase and pulled out a book. "Consider this a gift to you for all that you are going through."

The book was about fly-fishing for pike, a more esoteric outdoor activity. I was thrilled; I'm a fly-fisherman at heart. I had learned at a young age to drop a dry fly on the edge of a log without losing the fly. It was a simple but powerful gesture, a welcome act of kindness during a turbulent time. *Fly-fishing*, I thought. *That's just what I'll do.*

Establish Boundaries

I never dreamed of being a caregiver. When I had my first child, I knew many dirty diapers and potty training were in my future, but I hadn't thought I would one day be managing a bowel-and-bladder program for an adult. It was a difficult situation; I was happy to be there for her, but on the other hand, I would be lying if I said I wasn't uncomfortable with the new tasks I would have to perform. My coping mechanism was to treat it like anything else I had to do for her.

We established that Emily would be living with me after inpatient rehab; our next move was to determine who would do the caregiving. Emily was very comfortable with my helping her because I was family, which was convenient at first but only held her back in the end.

You may experience that your loved one prefers for you to help him or her with some of the activities that might be more embarrassing. It's important to your loved one to feel comfortable and secure, but it's even more important to help him or her regain independence.

My goal was to help Emily become more independent within two years, meaning, she could do some of her everyday activities on her own.

I remember when I told the nurses this at the hospital. They looked at me like I was an alien.

"Tall order, Jack," said one of the nurses. "It takes courage and patience to come this far, but now it is about commitment and hard work, and that will be up to your daughter." They were so right!

At times there was conflict and anger on both sides. Emily was still going through the grief stage, and some of those feelings of hopelessness wore me out. She would lash out for little reason, and all I could do was walk away for a short time to remove myself from the situation. Her being out of the hospital and rehab seemed to make it more real for Emily, and that only made recovery even more difficult. It was one of the hardest periods in my life, and it was certainly no cakewalk for my daughter.

Even though I had said two years, in my heart I prepared myself for a lifetime of emotional, financial, and personal commitment. In some regards, this is true for anyone. For any child, you are the greatest source of emotional support for the rest of your life. However, the goal is to help one stand strong on their own,

After we moved back home, it became harder for me to distinguish the line between my role of father and that of caregiver. My daughter became more and more reliant upon me. Even if it was a small task and we had a caregiver on duty, she would ask me to do it. I thought the attention would be helpful, but in time, I learned that it made it harder on my daughter, and on me as well.

I shared my experience with a friend I had recently met who had a brother who was a quadriplegic. She told me about her mother who was living with her quadriplegic brother and how this had created a codependency. It started becoming more and more difficult for both of them as the lines started to blur and expectations grew. Animosity and friction set in as the mother–son relationship started breaking apart. Many of my other new friends had warned me about this. The simple truth is that, when it comes down to it, it's hard to draw the line, but you must. Your relationship must stay whole, and that means you need to establish expectations up front and stick to them.

My greatest fear was that Emily would think I no longer helped with certain tasks because I didn't care. This couldn't have been further from the truth. The big picture was getting Emily to be independent, and that meant I needed to back further away. If Emily wanted to move back to Florida, it would give me peace of mind to know she was confident and in charge of her care. I had to create boundaries between our roles and, at the same time, make sure she started taking more responsibility for her journey.

Focus on the Big Picture

Spending so much time and effort on caregiving is exhausting. As parents, we often feel ashamed to admit when parenting becomes taxing; the same is true for caregiving. It's okay to feel negative every now and then. The solution to that negativity is to refocus on the big picture.

Emily and I bumped heads during her time living with me. There was a time Emily lost sight of what she was working toward, and I felt like I had to step in to help more often than was good for her. At the same time, I had issues going on in my own life. Work was difficult, and relationships were even more difficult. I had previously broken off an eight-year relationship because of these new responsibilities, including caring for my parents.

I felt as if I was being pulled in so many directions that it was wearing me down. It all culminated one night when Emily and I had an argument about the caregiver who was helping her. Emily didn't like the way she was handling her and wanted me to get rid of her. I felt like there was nothing more I could do; I really needed that help. I went down to the local pub just to visit with anyone and have a few cocktails to blow off steam. A few drinks were all it took before I realized this was not the answer to my problems. I needed to get Emily on a path to independence. Without her buy-in, she was destined to fail. And without having more space for myself, I was going to fail as well.

In time, we struck a balance. Emily's confidence in her abilities grew, along with her hope for the future. It was a very rough road getting there, but once you see your child achieving his or her dreams, all of those struggles seem to fade into the background.

There will be good days, and there will be not-so-good days. Keep in mind the goals you have and don't be hard on yourself if they aren't always in line with those of your loved one. And when all else fails, ask for help so you can remove yourself from the tasks and responsibly—even for a short time—to allow for refocusing on a positive plan.

Recovery Recap:

—Create balance between caregiving and relationships

—Communicate with your employer and stay engaged

—Enlist family and friends

—Take a break and don't lose yourself in the process

—Establish boundaries

—Empower your loved one to take control

—Focus on the big picture

Alex and Emily

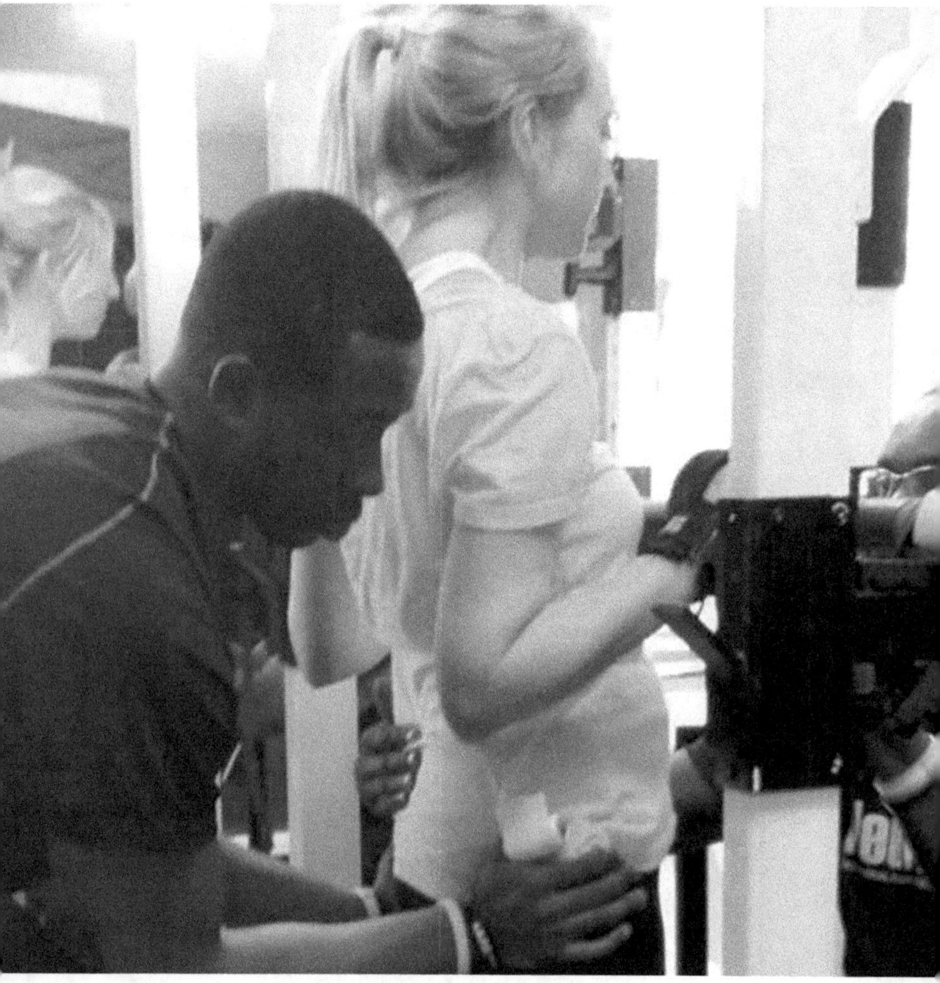

Standing at Rehab

CHAPTER 12

FINDING AND MANAGING CAREGIVERS

One of the most difficult tasks you will face once your loved one leaves the hospital is finding good, trustworthy, and caring caregivers. The next most difficult job is managing them and keeping them. In this chapter, I'll share with you how I found an excellent team of caregivers. In the next chapter, I'll detail how to organize and maximize their help.

We were lucky because the area in which we lived offered many career health-care programs in which prospective and active students were looking to gain experience and knowledge in working with a quadriplegic. Specifically, there was a local physician assistant program, which required a certain number of hours of related experience in the health-care field. What could be more educational than providing care to a recently injured quadriplegic? It was a good match for both Emily and the students.

Our first hire was bright, efficient, and engaged 100 percent of the time. As a rule, there was no reading books, watching TV, or sitting around waiting for direction. Once this caregiver learned the routine, she set out to improve it to the point where the task could be totally done within one and one-and-a-half hours, which to this day remains a record. Regretfully, this individual was getting ready to attend PA school after the summer ended, and so her time with us was short-lived. We learned from this caregiver that the type of helper we were looking for was someone who was compassionate and engaged and truly wanted to learn all aspects of improving the quality of life for my daughter.

Caregiver Basic Duties

In our case, a caregiver had to deal with medical concerns, hygiene, transportation, medical appointments, therapy, bowel-and-bladder management, picking up and organizing supplies and groceries, time management, and being supportive while encouraging independence.

We have come a long way from our first caregiver in terms of duties and activities. It still will change many times over, as Emily becomes more independent.

Credentials

Caregivers come with a wide range of experience and credentials. Some caregivers have no official credentials but have a great deal of experience. Others have caregiver credentials focused on primarily nonmedical tasks, like helping with bathing, dressing, meals, and housekeeping. These credentials include personal care assistant and home care assistant (PCA and HCA). Then there are credentials that include training on light medical assistance, such as help with medications and taking basic health-care measurements, such as temperature and blood pressure. These credentials include certified home health aide (CHHA), home health aide (HHA), restorative nursing assistant (RNA), and Certified Nursing Assistant (CNA).

More advanced credentials with additional requirements for education and licensing include the licensed practical nurse and licensed vocational nurse (LPN/LVN). The most formal credential for giving care is the registered nurse (RN), nurse practitioner (NP), physician assistant (PA) or medical doctor (MD) with precise state requirements for education, training, and licensing. The more medical help you and/or your loved one need, the more appropriate it is to look for credentials focused on medical issues and experience with similar conditions to those of you and/or your loved one.

For Emily, we chose private-care individuals with basic certification, such as CNAs. We made sure that they were current in both first aid and CPR. For medical needs, such as managing the bowel program and monitoring skin conditions and any other medical concerns, we utilized LPNs. For anything more medical related, we would take her to the internal medicine physician or the ER if we felt it was more critical.

Recruiting

Recruiting for talent is no easy task. Understand that you have two choices: agencies or direct hiring. If you choose agencies, your work is significantly less than if you hire direct. In either case, you need to create a job description and a list of activities that you require. This could include assisting with dressing, hygiene, showers, and so on. More importantly, there are personality traits that either make it a good fit or just not the right fit to propel your loved one forward with positivity.

We found that those who were optimistic and interested in learning about the injury were likely to be the most engaged and helpful. For my daughter, she needed someone to be engaged all the time, someone who wanted to truly learn about the best way to assist her and help her become more independent.

The best places to find prospects for direct care are Care.com, Indeed (indeed.com), health-care career boards, and on-site job postings. Care.com is mostly for those who have made caregiving their career and are looking for employment. Remember that the very best ones are most likely still working and not looking for employment however you may find one just getting off of an assignment. I suggest using your social network to ask if someone knows of a caregiver looking for work. One of the best places you can find someone is through a contact who can provide a solid reference.

Once you identify three or four individuals who appear to fit your needs, call them up and ask questions related to their experience, personality, and ability to succeed in the role of caregiver. The questions may include:

> —Have you ever worked with someone who is paralyzed?
>
> —What is your comfort level in learning?
>
> —Are you physically able to perform the duties?
>
> —Why do you want to do this kind of work?
>
> —What skills and experience will you bring to this role?

—What certifications do you have?

—How would you describe your organizational skills?

—Do you have a valid driver's license?

—Are you dependable and punctual?

—Are you okay with having a background check performed?

You can also do this with agencies as you interview the agency and caregiver. All you need to do is ask.

After the initial introduction, arrange to meet them in person with your loved one. Show them the job description and list of activities to be sure they understand what it will take. See if they click with your loved one, and even if they seem great, check their references and never make a decision to hire on the day of the interview. Think about it for at least twenty-four hours. If possible, arrange a two-hour training and trial session prior to committing to hire the individual.

To locate talent, one needs to be innovative, and that is why we went to nursing and medical schools, healthcare education websites, and even PA groups that were affiliated with universities. It was here that we found two additional individuals who were solid performers. Start thinking outside the box to capture the best of the best.

Agencies versus Private Care

When you work with agencies, you have a team of people looking after your loved one; however, consistency can be a real issue. In fact, to date, Emily still deals with lack of consistency-of-care issues on a semi-regular basis.

Should you choose to work with agencies, a good way to start is to first interview agencies in the area. This gives you an opportunity to meet with the leadership and find out more about what the agency can offer and its ability to communicate your needs to their staff. If you are considering using just agencies, then be sure to request that you meet with the same qualified individuals who would be taking care of your loved one and a commitment not to pull them from you for other cases that may require more hours. This happens more often than not.

Most agencies are looking for a steady schedule and not to be your "just-in-case" engagement. Many of the agencies we worked with in Michigan and Florida stated that they could help in a pinch, but when it came right down to it, most of them could not find anyone who could pick up a shift at a moment's notice. Realize that a majority of the caregivers from agencies have families and other commitments, so their time is limited for spur-of-the-moment requests. Make sure to pick two agencies at a minimum and use them consistently, even if it is every other weekend, to keep interest up in supporting you.

Hiring caregivers directly has its advantages, including discounted rates, more control, increased consistency, and increased efficiency; however, there are many more things that you are going to have to consider, such as payroll tax, insurance, liability, and adequate backup in the event one caregiver quits. In my opinion, the advantages of utilizing direct hire outweigh the disadvantages, but that does not mean you can't have both direct hires and agency workers.

Managing and Maintaining

Emily runs her caregivers as a business. She directly employs the caregivers, so she needs to have an Employer Identification Number (EIN) and be registered with the state for payroll. Each caregiver is required to clock in on Emily's computer, which makes payroll a lot easier. We ended up hiring a private payroll company to help process this, including paying taxes throughout each month. All we are required to do is send in the hours per employee, and in turn, we get the net amount for the paycheck. We chose to use a national bank and use direct deposit to pay caregivers every two weeks, which makes our lives easier.

When it comes to managing, the best approach is being direct and consistent and having clear expectations. In the next chapter, I'll cover how to do just that.

Recovery Recap:

—**Look for certifications, experience, and compassion.**

—**Recruit outside the box**

—**Utilize agencies for backup**

—**Interview with targeted objectives**

—**Have a monitoring system in place**

—**Set and follow through on expectations**

Out with Lauren

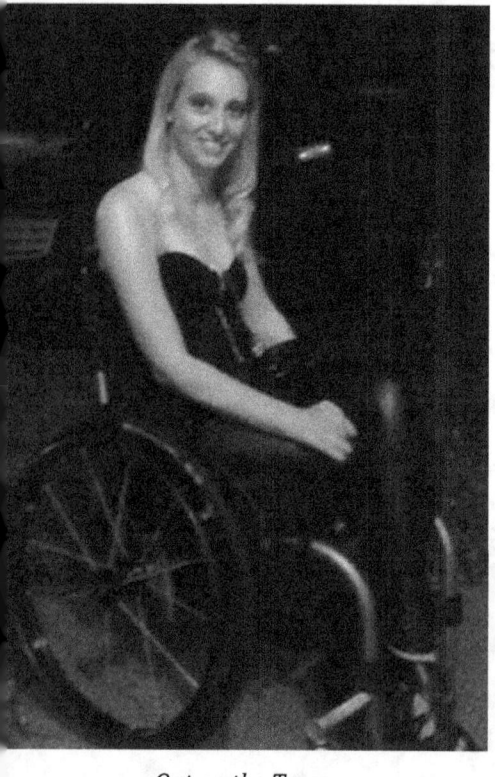

Out on the Town

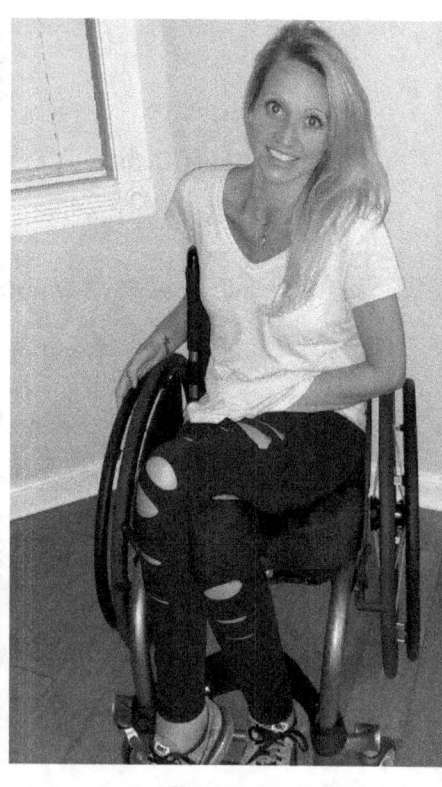

Ready to Go Somewhere

CHAPTER 13

CREATING YOUR CARE MANUAL

There is so much to learn and do when your loved one experiences a serious injury, but with focus, you can adapt and thrive. *I have learned that organization, coordination, and direction is crucial.* They also take a tremendous amount of time and energy.

If you can afford to hire one, a life coach with experience can help put processes in place and organize everything from daily activities to short- and long-term goals. This coach can help you and your loved one considerably. Otherwise, you may be the first one facilitating all of these factors until your loved one takes the helm. As a father with a career and significant responsibilities with my parents, I find this task daunting, but absolutely necessary.

My daughter doesn't accept all of my ideas or organizational skills. In fact, if I can sneak one in, I consider

> *I have learned that organization, coordination, and direction is crucial.*

myself very fortunate. My role is to listen and address the big problems. That continues to be my role to this day, to help with direction, but also to reduce her complicated life into a simple plan that she can manage. Keeping organization within her reach was helpful to assure consistency and expectations. I chose to create a "Team Emily Manual" that would have all the information together, in once place. I recommend that you do the same for your loved one.

To effectively keep track of therapy, doctors, caregivers, nutrition, and everything in between, where should you start?

Set Goals

Start defining short-term goals for the next thirty days for a starting point and then consider longer-term goals later on. When you reach thirty days, measure how you did and review what issues made it more difficult to reach some of your goals. Use that knowledge for your next set of goals. Remember to keep it simple, measurable and, most of all, achievable. Understand that some goals will change and that others will be discarded. This journey is long and undefined, so it's important to be patient.

Post a Schedule

Create a schedule with appointments and post it where everyone can see it, including your loved one. Post any scheduled activities that help others remember your priorities for the week, such as the thirty-day goals you defined. List the priority activities that caregivers or helpers should attend to on each particular day. Make sure to include doctors' appointments and therapy, and list which caregiver is working on that particular day or shift.

Create Caregivers' Expectations

If you want to achieve success in others who are caring for your loved one, it becomes imperative that you define and document the expectations up front and communicate them very clearly. By creating a simple list of expectations and posting it where everyone can see it, you can leave interpretation behind. You will also need to clearly communicate this verbally and frequently. In addition, it is helpful to create each caregiver's job description so that everyone understands who is responsible for what.

Define Home-Therapy Routines (Stretching, Range of Motion, Exercise)

Organize and document all of the stretching, range of motion, physical therapy, and occupational therapy activities that are performed at rehab so that they can continue at home. Realize that these will change continually as you see new therapists and trainers along the way but having something that you can work from to train others will be beneficial.

Create Your Ten-Point Caution List

Build your own ten-point list on what troubles to be on the lookout for. This can include both physical signals (e.g., pressure sores, redness, skin quality) and symptoms such as autonomic dysreflexia, along with how to address these issues. You should know what your loved one's baseline blood pressure and heart rate are so that you can compare results when something causes concern.

Document Medicines and a Care Team Contact List

Create a list of all the medications prescribed, including the brand name and generic name, dosage, what it is for, what it looks like, when it expires, and any special instructions. The care team contact list includes doctors, specialists, therapists, trainers, and caregivers. Be sure to include phone numbers and emails if they are made available.

Maintain a Daily Journal

Having a daily journal can be one of the most important documents you have. A journal helps with consistency and continuity of care. The important pieces of information that you record about daily activities and conditions can help with keeping track of issues or missed activities. Having a written history has always been very useful in addressing issues before they become a problem. In addition, a daily journal helps with consistency of care among all caregivers. This is the first thing they should look at before they start their shift to gain access to activities performed, demeanor, health concerns etcetera.

Build a Reference Library

Have available informative pamphlets and/or books to help caregivers understand more about the injury and methods of how to address the many aspects of spinal cord injury. I requested the *Paralysis Resource Guide* from the Christopher & Dana Reeve Foundation and many books from the Paralyzed Veterans of America. The amount and quality of information on the internet, especially through the Christopher & Dana Reeve Foundation, is exceptional. All of these publications are available in PDF format so you can download them for an iPad or tablet.

Procuring documents about the injury and support systems will help you learn more about caring for your loved one in addition to giving your caregivers a good start in understanding the best ways to provide care. Research online systems that can help organize this for you or create your own manual. Most importantly, keep it simple in every way, for simple is the best bet for success.

As a father and advocate for my daughter, I have striven to put systems in place that are easy to follow and simple for the caregivers. Because there is so much information to learn and remember, I chose to use CareZone (carezone.com) for a variety of reasons, but mostly because all the information that I've mentioned in building the care manual can fit into the application's site. The second most important reason was that my daughter could control access to all caregivers. It made perfect sense to have the information online, but it was equally important to have a hard copy at her home that anyone could pick up and review for information.

Recovery Recap:

—Set goals

—Build your care manual

—Post a daily activity schedule for caregivers

—Display caregiver expectations

—Post a monthly calendar (appointments)

—Define home therapy routines (e.g. stretching, ROM, exercises)

—Create your ten-point caution list (e.g. AD, pressure sores, rash, etc.)

—Maintain a daily journal (for caregivers to document in each shift)

—Share and display an updated medicine list and care-team contact info

—Build your own reference library

—Utilize online sources for scheduling and journalizing

Out for Dinner with Grandpa, Steve, Sue, Jack, and Emily

Standing with Nick at Barwis Methods

CHAPTER 14

IMMUNE SYSTEM AND NUTRITION

Most of us are aware of the importance of nutrition, but the focus seems to be more on the endless diets, fads, health benefits, and so on. Emily, like anyone else, needs the appropriate amount of proteins, carbohydrates, and fats. The difference is that now she needs those nutrients more than ever to maintain a healthy lifestyle.

Did you know that a quadriplegic requires 30 percent fewer calories than the average recommendation provides? Did you know that protein is more critical in increasing strength and helping build back muscle due to atrophy? Did you know that infection is one of the leading causes of death for those who have experienced a spinal cord injury?

These are reasons we need to dig a little deeper into the subject of nutrition and the immune system. This is a subject that I have a true affection for and have spent many years researching. There will always be opposing arguments, but by sticking with the basics, I hope we can make life a little easier and healthier for our loved ones who need strong immune systems more than ever.

Once in the hospital, there is a high risk of infection, so how can you protect your loved one? The common answer is to always use microbial soap and insist that each individual don a mask before entering the room, but there can be many other sources of infection, including the room itself.

Emily was regretfully diagnosed with MRSA during her inpatient rehab. Treating MRSA can be complicated and serious, and most importantly, it could have been prevented. It is known to be resistant to a certain type of antibiotics. If I had known about this serious infection regarding the risk, I would have called for extra precaution before she went into the hospital. After she was diagnosed with MRSA, every staff person who came in contact with her had to wear gloves, a mask, and a smock. It was burdensome, to say the least.

Not long after Emily moved in with me, she experienced many urinary tract infections from daily catherization's along with new issues surrounding her neurogenic bladder caused from the injury. We needed to address this and find new solutions for her infections. Once she was released from inpatient rehab, she met with a urologist about installing a port, called a Mitrofanoff, into her bladder, so she could catheterize herself without help. The doctor assured us that this was a very simple procedure. To install the port, the doctor would take Emily's appendix and use it as the "stoma," or port into the bladder. Because her bladder had shrunk significantly and no longer had the capacity, the urologist wanted to do a bladder augmentation at the same time. This surgery would give her the freedom and ability to empty her bladder without help and would reduce the amount of leakage she had been experiencing. It seemed complicated and risky; however, Emily was determined that this would assist her in her road to independence.

Emily had the surgery, and a few weeks later, there appeared to be some redness around the stoma. That redness developed into a small mass. Only a few days had passed when we noticed it had grown at a rate that caused concern. We decided to head to the ER once again to find out what was causing this new development. We were concerned that something had gone wrong with the surgery but learned from the urologist that this reaction was caused by a small infection around the stoma. The infection seemed to have created a hematoma (or blood mass) around the stoma.

The doctor in the ER made an incision around the protrusion to drain the hematoma. Now that the infection was present within, the incision would need to heal from the inside out, and so Emily took a course of antibiotics. Lucky me would have to "sterile pack" her wound (yet another arduous procedure) on a daily basis until it healed. Have you ever put on gloves that needed to stay sterile? I've got to hand it to the nurses who do this on a daily basis—this was another task that was more difficult for me a novice. What a process it was, and the worst part of it was that this went on for months. This was only the start of infections to come.

People who have experienced a spinal cord injury commonly develop urinary tract infections (UTIs), and Emily was no exception. She would get one just about every other month. The hospital treated it with antibiotics, but eventually, some of the medication became ineffective. What had caused it—her immune system? Or could it be the way she'd catheterized herself? I believe it was both; however, I did learn later on that she had had bladder stones that caused her autonomic dysreflexia. UTIs caused her to feel run down, sluggish, and nauseated. We eventually learned that one good precautionary measure whenever catheterizing is to use gloves and keep everything clean and sterile. This may seem obvious, but it's harder to manage than one might imagine.

When antibiotics are taken orally, they affect the gut in a most adverse way. These antibiotics can destroy much of the good bacteria. To battle the loss of the good bacteria, probiotics should be taken routinely. Many doctors and researchers agree that the gut has a direct correlation to the immune system. They are your immune system! To keep the body's immune system in balance, it is recommended that probiotics are taken as part of a daily regimen. It's important to have good bacteria but even more important, diversity of the good bacteria. Paying attention to your gut flora or gut microbiome is your ticket to better health which improves mood and reduces infection, disease, and inflammation.

Other factors that affect the immune system include lack of sleep, stress, exercise, and diet. Your first line of defense is to choose a healthy lifestyle. Getting enough sleep and keeping stress at bay can restore balance. A diet high in fruits and vegetables is another excellent preventative measure. These healthy foods contain antioxidants that help boost the immune system.

After a spinal cord injury, your body's systems, such as bowel, bladder, and skin, are altered due to paralysis. Because you are less active, your muscles and bones may become weaker. With less physical activity, you burn fewer calories and may gain weight and there can be an increased tendency to gain weight and heightened risk for osteoporosis (or loss of bone density) from the lack of bearing weight. Excess weight adds stress on your organs and will make transfers more difficult. This can also contribute to skin breakdown or pressure ulcers. Again, one thing that you can do to reduce some of these risks is to maintain a healthy diet.

Nutrition is even more important for individuals with spinal cord injuries as well as other serious medical conditions because of the increased risk for diabetes, vascular and heart disease, and obesity. Specific diet recommendations for spinal cord injuries include consuming lots of fiber (found in fruits, vegetables, and grains) and fluids to prevent constipation. The recommendation for daily fruit and vegetable intake is at least five servings per day. In addition, protein (lean meat, poultry, eggs, fish, and beans) should be added to the diet to continue to help build and maintain muscle and to help prevent pressure ulcers and preserve lean body mass. Choose a variety of high-protein foods that are lean and animals that have been fed a non-GMO diet. I would recommend either grass-fed beef, organic pasture raised chicken or wild caught fish. If you are trying to gain strength, you need additional protein for the building and recovery of muscles. You should take in fewer calories to balance lower energy use. By eating nutritionally balanced meals, you can give your body what it needs and lessen the chance of medical issues in the future.

    I find that all types of organic vegetables can help with not only delivering antioxidants but also with naturally providing your daily dosage of vitamins. This should be the number one place to focus on in providing good nutrition. I recommend mixing up the colors to provide variety and staying with local produce when it's available. Nothing helps your community more than buying local!

    Fruit is also big on my list but in moderation due to its high sugar content. The tropical fruits seem to have more sugar than apples, oranges, and strawberries, but with their fiber and vitamins, all fruits can be a much better choice than a candy bar. Remember to always choose organic when possible.

    I am a strong advocate of staying well away from sugar and soda in any form. Sugar is the number one killer and cause of diabetes and metabolic issues. If you can stay off the soda, you will be much better off. If you want to drink for health, try pure juice, such as cranberry or another low sugar fruit, and mix it with water. It may taste a little tart without all the sugar, but in time, you will get used to it. Drinking plenty of fluids also assists in fending off UTIs.

There's no better way to start the day than with a green veggie smoothie drink! Add a little protein powder, prebiotics with a bit of fruit to sweeten it, and away you go! Again, it may take some time to get used to it, but if you think about how it is helping your body fight for your health, it will soon start to taste much better.

Processed foods are just as deadly as sugar. When you can't pronounce an ingredient, or if the product has an endless list of ingredients, why would you want to eat it? Stay away from processed foods as much as possible to keep healthy. The sugar and sodium content alone is astronomical in some processed foods found on the shelves. Be smart, read the labels, and choose wisely, working toward whole-food choices.

Back when the "low-fat" label was in, people thought that fat content was making them fat. That couldn't be further from the truth! By maintaining a low-fat diet, we were essentially starving our brain of needed fats. What's even more interesting is the relationship now between Omega 3 and Omega 6. The typical diet that calls for Omega 6 versus 3 is way out of whack. The target needs to be 1:1 not 1:25. Where do you find Omega 3? You can find it in cold-water fish, fish oil, and grass-fed meats, along with fortified eggs. There are many opportunities to get your fats in balance. Plus, by learning more about food, you will learn more about how to make yourself think more clearly and feel better.

To stay fit and healthy, eat whole foods, quality protein, good fats and stay away from processed foods, soda, and sugar. By eating intentionally and understanding your dietary needs, you will perform and feel better all the way around.

Recovery Recap:
—Practice good hygiene.

—Reduce stress.

—Get adequate sleep.

—Take probiotics and prebiotics

—Eat more organic vegetables and fruits

—Consume quality protein

—Remove processed foods

—Reduce sugars and soda

—Increase Omega 3 over Omega 6

Jack, Emily, and Mike Barwis

Emily, Dan, and Brian at Barwis Methods

CHAPTER 15

THERAPY FOR LIFE

Just as nutrition is important for healing, exercise is the cure for a multitude of ailments let alone keeping us healthy! A catastrophic injury can create barriers for keeping one in shape, but Emily learned to overcome them. First and foremost, therapy and exercise should be an absolute for anyone with a spinal cord injury. From stretching and range of motion, to massage and exercise, there is little in your way except time.

I believe that my daughter will walk again in her lifetime, and I want to be sure to give her every opportunity to make that a reality. Stretching and daily exercise are her two greatest tools. The thought of daily exercise might be intimidating, but consider the alternative: if you don't contract those muscles every day, they will atrophy. When the next technology evolves, Emily could be ready to leave that chair behind! So where do you start?

Emily and I first learned the basics of stretching legs, arms, shoulders, feet, hands, and fingers in the hospital. We made it a twenty-minute daily regimen in the morning, partly while she was in bed and an evening session as well. Once we understood stretching and range of motion (ROM), we learned more advanced stretches and exercises to further prevent her muscles from losing tone and flexibility.

Performing ROM seemed to help Emily with her leg spasms. These spasms are typically treated with medication, but Emily has always been one to take the least amount of medication she needs due to side effects such as fatigue and lack of drive. One interesting feature of these spasms was that they kept her legs looking fit with good tone. For her, it was bittersweet because even though her legs had retained tone and definition, they were heavy, and that meant more difficult transfers for her and for us when we assisted.

With spasms comes stiffness and reactions when you stretch, this can be difficult to work with. Before, we used to fight the spasm while stretching. Now we just let the spasm work through the stretch by applying less pressure.

Since being out of rehab, Emily has participated in many types of advanced therapies to help her gain strength for transfers and many other tasks. This includes certain muscle groups even below the injury line, such as her abdomen. The muscles seem to have a way to engage even though they may have lost their connection to the brain.

One of the most important pieces of information that I learned is that the mind is responsible for 90 percent in regained function. If you want to regain more function, you first must believe it is possible, and then you need to practice thinking about it over and over. The mental toughness and psychological approach you take are up to you and your team. Believe in it, and it can happen.

While Emily was in rehab, a therapist recommended "e-stim," or electrical stimulation for helping contractions to regain strength in targeted muscles. It stimulates the muscles between two points and creates a contraction within the muscle. This helps keep the muscle from atrophying.

Be careful, though, for you can create some pretty strong reactions. The e-stim therapy was quite involved, as I had to understand where and what each muscle group was, both visually and by touch. Even though I was up for the challenge, I did not have the time or knowledge to do this on my own, so I chose working with an experienced and knowledgeable therapist.

When Emily received her first grant for therapy, it was at a facility called The Recovery Project. The facility was created to help those with neurological diseases, spinal cord injury, or traumatic brain injury. This place is top-notch. When we went to her first therapy session, we were met by two of the owners, Charlie Parkhill and Polly Swingle. After sustaining a spinal cord injury, Charlie was told that he would never walk again. Polly started working at a rehab center with Charlie and believed that with a high-intensity protocol, he could regain function. Charlie not only regained function but also was able to walk one hundred feet unassisted after being in a chair for years. Inspired by these results, the two founded The Recovery Project in 2003.

The therapy grant allowed Emily to participate in therapy twice a week for three months. I learned about the rehab facility through one of the many new relationships at rehab and called to find out more. Polly ended up calling me back right away. She told me to fill out an application for the grant that the center was trying to fill before the end of the year. Yet another wonderful surprise only months after Emily's accident. How timely it was! Our faith just grew even stronger.

We started in just two months after our applications was submitted and met our team at The Recovery Project, the physical therapist and trainer. At first, Emily worked on a standing frame to start getting her body used to standing at least weekly. Then they went right to helping with her transfers. She was able to experience ambulating using the Lokomat on a weekly basis. This was her first step toward knowing that the possibilities for recovery were endless. She also worked on an e-stim bike that activated contractions in her quads to simulate pedaling on a bike. There she was on a stationary bike pedaling on her own. Her trainer worked on her strength and endurance with weights and other more basic types of equipment. Thanks to The Recovery Project, she was well on her way!

It was not long after the Recovery Project that we moved onto Barwis Methods therapy. Mike Barwis has an extraordinary amount of knowledge about the mechanics and strength of the body. When he explained how a muscle contracts and releases, I knew we were in the right place. He personally worked with Emily in the beginning, and then Dan Moses took the helm as her trainer. After working on a weight bench with her arms, Dan had her try to do crunches. For a while it seemed as if only her shoulders were doing the work; however, Dan felt there was slight ab activation. Dan continued to push her in areas that were new to her. Most impressive was the air weight machine to assist her in performing squats. While one person was holding her hands on the bar protecting her wrists and the other person was working the controls, she would be lowered down and then up with the air control while she would engage and visualize her shoulders, abs, and any other muscle group to assist the squat routine. She would be reminded to concentrate on her leg and abdomen muscles during the exercise to help try to build a connection back to the brain. Once they placed her on the artificial-turf floor on her stomach, she was told to do many modified push-ups again to help work those abs. She spent the next year working with them until she moved to

Florida. Her luck followed her, as the Barwis Methods group opened a facility less than an hour away from her Florida home. What appreciation we both have for the Barwis community!

Once Emily was down in Florida, it was just a few months later that she was invited by Susan Harkama to the University of Louisville to participate in a few case studies including an epidural-stimulation study. Remember the tennis ball? We were sure to make it down there to see Dr. Harkama in the very least. When we arrived, the staff swiftly got us started with test after test along with a lengthy explanation of what each test was about. Then the real cool stuff was about to begin! She was fitted with a harness that enabled her to walk with one person on each side, working her legs on a treadmill. They placed dozens of reflectors on her legs and put her on a treadmill that had an array of cameras recording her gait. They also had her fitted with sensors to record her breathing, heartbeat, blood pressure, and muscle contractions to understand what percentage of muscles were doing any of the work. It was amazing to watch the visual of the reflectors on the monitor that showed her steps as she walked! Watching her gait on a computer screen reminded me how she had walked before, and the most exciting part was that many of her leg muscles were contracting or assisting her. The muscles actually seem to have a memory to them, even without a connection back to the brain. This was another one of those awe-inspiring moments felt by both of us.

So many opportunities seemed to come our way because I wasn't afraid to let Emily's story be known.

Therapy has so many different options that you can choose. Some programs offer basic function enhancement and adaptive strategies to help one gain further independence. Others focus on maintaining muscle tone and development of strength and endurance. Then there are the advanced programs that are looking for the next cure or adaptive device that can change the playing field. Each area is important, so do your research and be sure to include the most appropriate and beneficial therapy program.

You will need to understand that each program has its own purpose and is all-important to the health of the individual. Essential to each of them is the team you select. Utilizing personal trainers can help one gain muscle and endurance. Physical therapists and occupational therapists help one regain function and learn new methods through adaptation. There are many new, more advanced therapies available coming online every day, and we will continue to seek a cure. Always keep the hope alive!

Recovery Recap:

—**Learn to stretch and exercise every day**

—**Seek therapy programs in your area**

—**Stay current with new and upcoming rehabilitation strategies**

—**Get involved with studies**

—**Explore sports therapy opportunities**

—**Research therapy grants and special funding**

—**Explore new ways to adapt and live**

AACIL Benefit

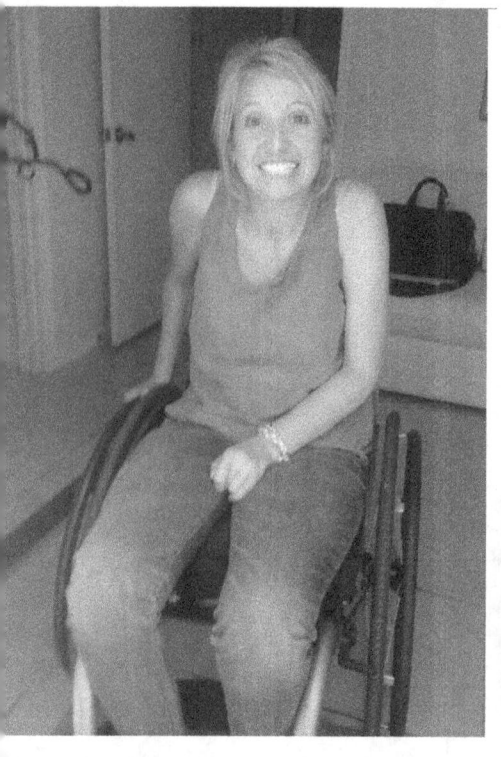

Emily Moves to FL

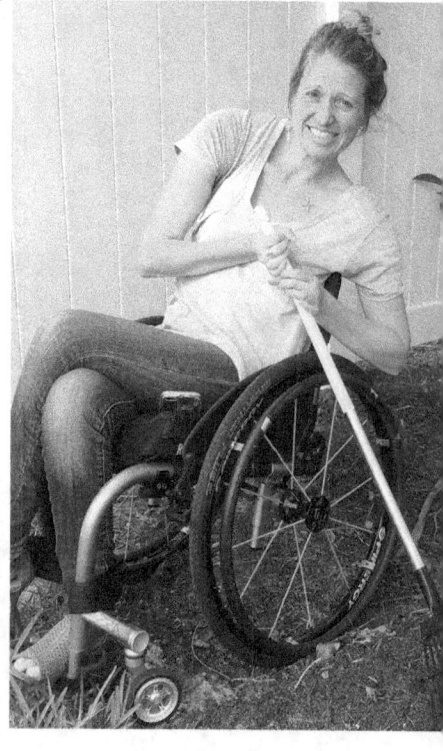

Emily Landscaping at Home

CHAPTER 16

NEXT STEP TO INDEPENDENCE

Preparing for independence means a lot for a quadriplegic. It means he or she has overcome tremendous obstacles and fought a hard-won battle. It means he or she has reached a stable place in which to feel comfortable being responsible for his or her own care, including staying on top of health, nutrition, and exercise and managing caregivers. It also means there's an incredibly exciting, and frightening, transition that will soon take place.

Your loved one has spent countless hours rehabilitating and adapting through the support of family, friends, and a team of specialists. When he or she is finally prepared to return to some form of independence, the revelation can be both exhilarating and scary.

And that's exactly how I felt when Emily realized she was ready. I was so proud of everything she had accomplished, and yet the idea of moving her to Florida was unthinkable. But the time had come.

It had been two-and-a-half years since the accident, but it felt more like months. As Emily adapted to her new abilities, I adapted to having her at home. Packing up Emily's belongings felt more like emptying the house. There was hardly any time to process everything; once she had decided she was ready, it was just a short matter of time before we had arranged a caravan to move her down south.

Emily couldn't contain her excitement for the transition, but deep down, I think we both sensed the fear we had, along with the sadness, knowing we would both miss each other. The night before our departure, I stayed up after Emily went to bed and cleaned the house. I've never liked to come home to a disorganized, unclean place. Emily is the same; she has always wanted to keep things in order, which is good because now, more than ever, it would be a necessity for her care.

When I finally did go to bed, I was restless. While everyone else was asleep, it suddenly dawned on me that I was sending my daughter into a world of unknowns. Her new roommate was an old coworker she had known for years, but from my perspective, she had no idea what living with a quadriplegic would truly be like. Would she be able to deal with the transition? Would their friendship survive? I tried to stay optimistic.

I created a budget for all the expenses that she would be responsible for. Her SSA income barely covered part of the rent, so I would be subsidizing it, including medical expenses, caregivers, housing, groceries, and the rest.

I had posted an ad on care.com looking for caregivers in the area, and once I got down there, I would interview those who had replied to the job posting. I also reached out to a few doctors to be sure that we had one set up before we arrived. I would need to evaluate the housing situation that her roommate had picked out and make any changes to allow her mobility in the home and, more important, to keep her safe. I thought we had everything in order, for the most part; however, there would be many holes in our execution.

We had arranged to have Emily's caretaker travel with us so she could train the roommate and other caregivers who would be helping Emily. But what if we couldn't find a good match? What if something happened and I wasn't down the hall to help? Could we get the two shifts that we needed?

When you find yourself plagued with the 2 a.m. "what-ifs," all you can do is take a deep breath and remind yourself of all the hard work leading up to this day. Put faith in your loved one. After all, he or she has made it this far.

The morning came fast, and I got up early to meet the caregiver who was making the trip with us. She was one of the better caregivers we had the good luck of finding. She was patient, easygoing, and had a knack for dealing with Emily. She had been working with my parents for almost a year before I brought her on to help with Emily, so she knew more about my family history and all its trials and tribulations than perhaps even I did.

It would be a grueling two-day drive, and we could use all the support we could get. Sure enough, the morning we awoke, the van had a flat tire, and the U-Haul trailer had issues with the trailer hitch and lights. After the tire was repaired, the next stop was the U-Haul depot to get that fixed. Hours later, we were finally on the road. It was at this strategic moment that Emily decided she wanted to stop at Starbucks. One hour-long detour later, we were officially on our way, and the eleven-hour road trip had commenced.

I headed up the caravan in the moving truck, and the caregiver drove the van behind us. I had this harebrained idea that we could drive straight down to Florida, but I was with others that seemed to be drinking a significant amount of fluids, so that wasn't going to happen. Emily had to be catheterized every four hours, and everyone wanted to stretch, so we had to make several stops along the way.

Many hours later and multiple stops for food, drink, and bathroom breaks, we were close to half the distance to

Florida, and it was time to find a hotel to bed down. We were all ready to get into the horizontal position, and soon we found a place that worked well.

The next morning, everyone was up, and we were on the road by 9 a.m. We made it out of the mountains, and I was relieved to see a long, flat horizon all the way down to Florida. With many stops along the way and at least ten hours on the road, we finally made it to West Palm Beach. We made our first big milestone however there were surprises just around the corner.

When we first pulled in, we were to meet the landlord, along with Emily's roommate, and do a walkthrough of the house. It was a three-bedroom house that was not best suited for her by any means. It was dirty and not located in the ideal area for my daughter. Her new roommate had picked out the place, and one would think that she would have experienced the same thoughts when she had first walked through it.

Of course, the roommate was nowhere to be found and wasn't answering her phone. We ended up paying the first month's rent and were handed the keys before the roommate even showed up. When she did, she looked like she was in rough shape; she had been at a wedding the night before and hadn't gotten any sleep.

What have I gotten my daughter into? I thought. Emily had pushed hard for this to happen, and so I decided to support her, but I was more than cautiously concerned.

As we moved the furniture in and emptied out the two trucks, things started falling into place. The roommate was in school to become an RN. That seemed to calm the situation at hand until I tried to get her to spend some time with the caregiver whom I had brought down with me. The roommate ended up not moving in until right after the caregiver had left and believed that she could handle it on her own without any training. She was absolutely clueless!

When I left for Michigan, I could only imagine all of the potential disasters that could occur. Ultimately, I needed to have my daughter take responsibility, and maybe this would help her become even more independent. It turned out that the roommate left halfway through the lease, without providing any notification. Lucky for Emily and me, Emily had a boyfriend at the time, who ended up moving in with her to help out. It gave me comfort, knowing that someone was there with her in the evening.

Looking back, I see there were principal steps I had missed that would have helped make Emily's transition between living with her father and becoming responsible for her own care much smoother. Of course, some things will arise that you perhaps didn't consider. The most important step is to be sure your loved one has a network of support for whatever comes his or her way.

Establish Care Providers (Doctors, Caregivers, Therapists)

By this point, you have established some kind of medical insurance or coverage to handle medical care. Be sure your loved one understands their coverage and limitations so that they are better equipped to handle their care once they are on their own.

If moving to another area, it would be very helpful to have an experienced doctor on your team prior to moving so he or she can help you at a moment's notice. For my daughter, we ended up finding an internal medicine doctor who could help with her care and assisted us in finding a medical facility that was close to her new home.

Most important, is to determine the new caregivers who are going to be part of the routine. Make sure you have someone you can trust who is reliable, honest, experienced, and caring and is not bringing any drama or other issues into your loved one's life.

Establish a Budget

Most likely, you have been handling all of the bills since the time of the accident. As you get a better sense of the financial support that will be in place for your loved one, it's important to have guidelines for how much can be spent, and on what. Medical prescriptions and doctors' bills will be a critical part of your budget. The caregivers, on the other hand, may be your greatest expense. Create a budget for both discretionary and nondiscretionary items. Know which are the most important to keep your loved one safe and healthy.

Educate your loved one on the priority areas for care and the costs associated with them. He or she is, in essence, responsible for sticking to a budget no matter who is funding it.

Research Accessibility in the New Home

Before purchasing any new equipment, it is critical that you visit the new home. Check for accessibility, from thresholds to doorways, to be sure that your loved one can safely get into the home or rooms without issue. Examine how the bathrooms are set up and what is needed to make them usable and accessible. The kitchen is another important room in which you want to determine accessibility to the cupboards, refrigerator, and stove. After two-and-a-half years of Emily living with me, I understood what I was looking for, and even if it were temporary, we could make it work. It is all based on the individual, but more important, you will need to visualize the present needs and the needs of the future, for it will change.

Utilize Your Social Network

Emily's Florida friends were busy now, most often with their work and relationships. They were all so good to her while she was still in Florida, but after two-and-a-half years, she had lost contact with most of them. My hope was that they would come to see her once she was back in Florida. Maybe they could pick up where they'd left off. Either way, it was important that Emily had people around her. If your loved one is moving to a place where he or she may not know many people, be proactive in helping him or her make connections with new friends and establish a new network. I ended up meeting with both of her neighbors to explain her situation. They both offered to help anytime she needed them, which was a relief for me.

Church was yet another great place to access new friends and become more connected to the area. Fortunately, Emily had a church that she had regularly attended before her accident, so there was a support system close by if she needed it. Even though the living situation was a far cry from my expectations, the church did give me additional comfort.

Appreciate the Past; Look Forward to the Future

As her move came to a close, I was flooded with bittersweet feelings as I wondered what was in store for Emily. I would miss her and her company, but I wouldn't quite miss all the caregivers who were always around. It would be nice to have the place to myself and back in order. When the accident first occurred, I had no idea where I would find the time to manage everything going on in my life; now, years later, it was time to get back to my "new normal" life, whatever that would be.

Maybe I would travel to see my kids and grandkids more often and go on additional mission trips. Maybe I would make my way back to Colorado and hike more of the "fourteeners," or just get back to focusing on my life and possibly even having a girlfriend again. Anything seemed possible at the time.

Recovery Recap:

—**Establish care providers (doctors, caregivers, therapists)**

—**Establish a budget**

—**Research accessibility for any new living environment**

—**Recruit and train caregivers**

—**Utilize your social network for support**

—**Appreciate the past and look toward to the future**

Emily, Ashley, and Dad at Grandma Isabelle's Memorial

Ashley, Emily, and Dad at a Basketball Game

Epilogue

Once I found myself caring for my daughter, I knew that my purpose in life had expanded well beyond myself. I have such gratitude for everything that God has helped me work through and, most important, the relationships that he has put within reach, many of which have created new possibilities for Emily's road to recovery.

I have been fortunate with my job and those who have supported me throughout this journey. When I was asked to join this special team, "Team Emily," I did not understand how important it was to those who are also dealing with the tremendous stress and obstacles involving rehabilitation and recovery after a catastrophic injury. But I do now, and I will continue to tell this story of triumph and how we can all be an inspiration to others. This became my true purpose, and it remains so to this day.

Today, Emily lives by herself and leads a full life. She has many friends; she did lose some, but she has made many new friends and has had a few boyfriends, too. She has learned to clean, cook, and perform many small tasks without assistance. For those chores with which she still needs help, she has caregivers who assist her in the morning and at night. I am still working on coordinating care with help, but it is much less challenging, as she has taken on much of this management. She has returned to school part-time and is working toward a degree in nutrition. She purchased a home that has an open floor plan with an outdoor courtyard that she spends a good amount of time in. She has learned to adapt her home space to meet her needs, a process that is still evolving. She recently purchased a Jeep and at this point is the passenger but soon it will be time for her to get her license. Then again, an automatous jeep may be her next step to independence.

Emily's next goals include working toward being able to transfer to and from her chair on her own. Exercise is very important to her as she continues to work out on her NuStep every day for more than an hour, go to therapy bi-weekly, and take her daily strolls (in her favorite chair) with her dog. She understands the healing power of nutrition and continues to make good choices related to her eating habits. With all the business of life, it still is an ongoing battle for her, as it is for us. Her strength and endurance continue to increase from her therapy and her constant workouts. This endurance is reflected in her ability to spend time cleaning her home and doing her own laundry. Just recently, Emily made multiple transfers from her chair to the bed all by herself, another one of those "proudest days" of her life. It may have not looked the prettiest, but it was another leap towards what she will be able to do in the near future.

Emily's support system is growing, and she has continued to ask for the quality care she requires for staying healthy. She can be demanding and more detail specific given her world is different from most of ours. I am so proud of the progress she has made. We are all fortunate for all the lessons we have and can learn from her. Her determination, perseverance, kindness, patience, and faith are strong examples of how one can take a situation and turn it into a positive opportunity.

No matter what the present challenges reveal, both Emily and I have faith that she can overcome and find the best for years to come. If you ever run into her, you will be able to see first hand the many great qualities she has and the positive outlook on life she practices every day.

I have hope that you, too, can find the answers and solutions that will help you and your loved one overcome unplanned challenges whenever and whatever they may be. Remember that challenges are opportunities in disguise and that when you see one door close, others open if you continue to look for the open door. Know that the love, positive attitude, and drive you summon will help you and those around you in this wild ride called "life."

Go, Team Emily!

May you have days full of blessings and abundance as you embark on your journey.

Birthday at the Gym

At Dad's Office with Max

Barwis with Nick

Emily and Grandma Isabelle

Emily and Stella

Eating Out in PBG

Emily's Brother Josh, Christine, Emily, and Dad

Family Picture in Michigan

Garver, Isabelle, Dad, and Emily in NPB

First Visit Back to FL

With Grandpa in NPB

Sip and Paint Fun

Out with Friends

Uncle Steve and Emily

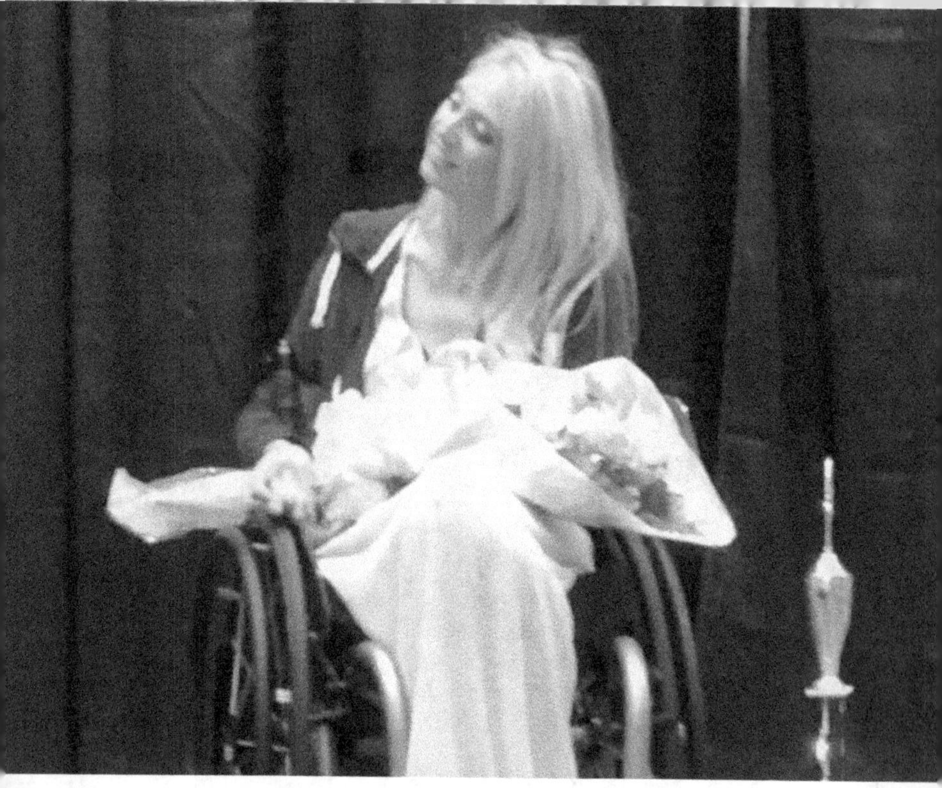

Third Runner up in Ms. Wheelchair Florida 2017

Emily and Dad at Dinner

Ready to Go Out on the Town

Additional Resources

—National Institute of Health

—Spinal Cord Injury Information

—American Paraplegia Society

—International Spinal Cord Society

—Model SCI Systems Dissemination Center

—National Organization on Disability

—University of Michigan

—Paralysis Community (a resource of the Christopher & Dana Reeve Foundation with a safe and secure online social networking site containing a robust discussion area on many areas of paralysis, including caregiving)

—Caregiver Action Network (educates, supports, and empowers families who care for chronically ill, aged, or disabled loved ones)

—National Alliance for Caregiving (coalition of national groups that supports family caregivers and the professionals who help them)

—The Rosalynn Carter Institute for Caregiving (establishes local, state, and national partnerships committed to promoting caregiver health, skills, and resilience)

—<u>Caregiving.com</u> (Web community for families and healthcare professionals who care for chronically ill or disabled family members)

—<u>The Family Caregiver Alliance</u> (FCA) (operates the National Center on Caregiving to develop support programs for family caregivers in every state)

—<u>AARP</u> (caregiving resource center, including legal issues, long-distance caregiving, and end-of-life issues)

—<u>Today's Caregiver</u> magazine (topic-specific newsletters, online discussion lists, chat rooms, and an online store)

—<u>National Respite Coalition Network</u> (helps parents, caregivers, and professionals take a break, using respite services in their local area)

—<u>National Caregivers Library</u> (source of free information for caregivers)

—<u>Shepherd's Centers of America</u> (SCA) (interfaith organization that coordinates nearly one hundred independent Shepherd's Centers across the United States to help older adults remain independent)

—<u>Hiring and Management of Personal Care Assistants for Individuals with SCI</u> (downloadable booklet from the SCI Project at Santa Clara Valley Medical Center. Covers everything from locating and hiring to training and paying personal assistants. Includes forms, checklists, and resources)

—<u>CareCure Forum</u> (active forum and helpful message board for loved ones and caregivers of people living with paralysis)

—<u>Spinal Cord Injury Caregivers</u> (forum on Yahoo to share information and support other caregivers who are caring for people with SCI)

www.ingramcontent.com/pod-product-compliance
Lightning Source LLC
Chambersburg PA
CBHW070040230426
43661CB00034B/1444/J